The
Canadian Barbecue
Cookbook

Brad Smoliak • Jean Paré

Pictured on front cover: Teriyaki-glazed Ribs, p. 56

The Canadian Barbecue Cookbook

First Printing June 2012

Library and Archives Canada Cataloguing in Publication

Smoliak, Brad, 1966-

The Canadian barbecue cookbook / Brad Smoliak, Jean Paré.

(Canada cooks)

Includes index.

At head of title: Company's coming.

ISBN 978-1-897477-81-6

1. Barbecuing--Canada. 2. Cookbooks. I. Paré, Jean, 1927-

II. Title. III. Series: Canada cooks series

TX840.B3S62 2012   641.5'784   C2011-907083-9

Portions of this book were previously published by Lone Pine Publishing as *The Canadian Barbecue Cookbook*, 2008. Company's Coming recipes contributed by Jean Paré: Bourbon Chicken Wings, Prosciutto Pork Mignon with Parsley Cilantro Crema, Romano Ciabatta Vegetable Salad, Coconut Pesto-stuffed Chicken Breasts, Blue Cheese Beer Burgers, Seared Tuna Steak with Sesame Ginger Sauce, Smoked Fennel Trout, Orange Chili-stuffed Pork Chops and Spiced Grilled Peaches.

Published by

Company's Coming Publishing Limited

2311 – 96 Street

Edmonton, Alberta, Canada T6N 1G3

Tel: 780-450-6223   Fax: 780-450-1857

www.companyscoming.com

Company's Coming is a registered trademark owned by Company's Coming Publishing Limited

We acknowledge the financial support of the Government of Canada through the Canada Book Fund for our publishing activities.

Printed in China

CONTENTS

The Company's Coming Legacy

Jean Paré grew up with an understanding that family, friends and home cooking are the key ingredients for a good life. A busy mother of four, Jean developed a knack for creating quick and easy recipes using everyday ingredients. For 18 years, she operated a successful catering business from her home kitchen in the small prairie town of Vermilion, Alberta, Canada. During that time, she earned a reputation for great food, courteous service and reasonable prices. Steadily increasing demand for her recipes led to the founding of Company's Coming Publishing Limited in 1981.

The first Company's Coming cookbook, *150 Delicious Squares*, was an immediate bestseller. As more titles were introduced, the company quickly earned the distinction of publishing Canada's most popular cookbooks. Company's Coming continues to gain new supporters in Canada, the United States and throughout the world by adhering to Jean's Golden Rule of Cooking: Never share a recipe you wouldn't use yourself. It's an approach that has worked—millions of times over!

A familiar and trusted name in the kitchen, Company's Coming has extended its reach throughout the home with other types of books and products for everyday living.

Though humble about her achievements, Jean Paré is one of North America's most loved and recognized authors. The recipient of many awards, Jean was appointed Member of the Order of Canada, her country's highest lifetime achievement honour.

Today, Jean Paré's influence as founding author, mentor and moral compass is evident in all aspects of the company she founded. Every recipe created and every product produced upholds the family values and work ethic she instilled. Readers the world over will continue to be encouraged and inspired by her legacy for generations to come.

INTRODUCTION

One of my favourite pastimes is barbecuing and grilling.

What is the difference?

Barbecuing is basically low and slow—300° F (150° C) or lower—with the lid closed and with the smoke as a flavouring. Large, tougher cuts of meat are usually used for barbecuing.

Grilling is typically what most of us do with smaller, more tender cuts such as our steaks, chops, burgers, etc. Grilling uses a much higher heat. The heat can come from natural gas, propane or charcoal.

It doesn't matter what kind of barbecue you have. The techniques can be adapted to anything from a campfire in the woods to a fancy stainless steel number in a high-end outdoor kitchen.

What's important is the ingredients: search out the best meats, fish, vegetables, fruits, cheeses, wines, beers—whatever—you can find locally and in season. Go to farmers' markets and talk to the farmers and producers to find out what's out there. You'll find that it's easy to adapt the recipes to what's available and what your family likes.

Equipment and Tools

For all the recipes used in this book, I used a gas barbecue. If I had used propane, there would have been very little difference in the cooking processes, other than the fire burning a little hotter.

Many barbecues now come with fire starters. If your barbecue does not have a side burner, take a trip to an Asian market and buy a portable gas burner and refill cartridges for less than 50 bucks. They work great!

Tools

Single-use tools and gadgets are not my cup of tea. Some are not well made, some you will rarely use, and all of them just take up space. Here is a list of tools that you will need.

Spray Bottle: Fill it with water to control flare-ups, or to put out burning cedar planks. I also have a spray bottle filled with canola oil so I can oil my grill and tools, so that food will not stick to the grill.

You can also put apple cider in a spray bottle to add moisture to meats like pork during the cooking process.

Metal Tongs: If treated well they will last a long time. Use them for picking up meats, turning items, and moving smoking packages.

Wire Brush: Get a good sturdy wire brush that has long bristles to reach in between the grills. Brush your grill after you're preheated the barbecue but before you put the food on, and then again after each use.

Instant-read Thermometer: All the recipes here suggest cooking times, but there are so many variables involved with barbecuing and grilling here in Canada. Weather is the biggest variable. That steak you grill in July will take less time than when you grill it in October.

These thermometers take mere moments to give you a temperature reading—that's why they're called "instant-read."

Metal Spatula: Pick something sturdy to flip burgers, fish, etc.

Silicon Basting Brush: I like silicon brushes better than nylon brushes. They are easier to clean, and they don't melt as easily.

Optional

Skewers: Metal is better, but if you use bamboo, make sure you soak them in water for at least 30 minutes so they don't catch fire on the grill.

Apron: For the times that very hot spatters of sauce or oil leap from the grill.

Small saucepan: For sauces. Use it on the side burner or right on the grill.

Large fork, or pigtail: For turning large items when you need two hands.

A cast iron skillet and untreated cedar planks will round out your gear.

The Basics

Salt

Salt is needed to bring out the flavour of the food, so make sure you use it liberally. I recommend kosher salt for basic everyday grilling. It is coarser and has better flavour than ordinary table salt, and it is easier to use because of the larger crystals.

One quick way to spice up your grilling repertoire is to try different salts. For example, smoked salt, Hawaiian salt and *fleur de sel* all offer subtly different flavours.

Clean the Grill

Clean and oil your grill each time after you've finished barbecuing, and do the same before using it again. Preheat the barbecue first, then clean and oil the grills.

Heat the Grill

Getting the grill hot is another key to food not sticking. The grill is one of the first pieces of equipment turned on in a restaurant.

Also remember that not everything needs to be grilled over high setting.

If you don't have a thermometer on your barbecue, here's how to tell how hot it is:

Low heat: you can hold your hand over the burner for 7 to 10 seconds

Medium heat: you can hold your hand over the burner for 5 to 7 seconds

High heat: 2 to 3 seconds or you lose your eyebrows.

Dry the Food

Make sure that the food you put on the grill is patted dry. If there is any water or moisture left on it, your food will steam, not grill.

Food Safety

Make sure that the food to be barbecued stays cold until ready to grill or barbecue. The exception to this rule is beef, which should be allowed to reach room temperature before you place it on the grill.

Make sure you use a clean set of tongs or utensils when handling raw meats, especially chicken, so as to not transfer possible raw juices to the cooked product.

If you've marinated or brined meat, discard the marinade or brine; do not use it to baste the meat on the barbecue. If you want to use the marinade for the cooked food, reserve a quantity in a separate container before you marinate.

Techniques

Grill Marks

Grill marks are produced when you rotate, or turn, the item so it continues to cook on the same side but the hot grill creates an attractive cross-hatch charring pattern.

When your grill is hot and well oiled, and the food is ready for the barbecue, place the item on the grill. Grill for the amount of time indicated in the recipe, and then rotate the item 90° on the grill. Cook as indicated in the recipe, then flip the item over and repeat the steps.

To "flip" the item is to turn it from raw side up to raw side down.

Smoking

Smoking was first used to preserve meat, but now it is used more as a flavouring, giving the home chef another dimension. You want to use hardwood, and fruit tree woods are particularly good because they add subtle flavour to the food. If you have a fruit tree in your backyard, save the pruned branches for the barbecue. Simply chop the branches into smaller pieces and soak before using as smoking chips. These fresh "homegrown" chips will have more flavour than those found in stores.

Soak Chips: Choose a flavour that you like and soak chips for at least 30 minutes in water so they don't just burn up in a flash in the barbecue.

I use apple wood and cherry wood chips because I like the subtle flavour added to the meat, but you can use any other hardwood such as mesquite or hickory if you can find it.

Don't ever use softwood chips in the smoker: an unpleasant flavour is imparted to the meat.

Prepare Your Foil Smoking Pouch: For each smoking pouch, take a square of heavy foil and place about a cup of soaked wood chips in the middle of the square. Gather up the corners of the square and seal firmly. Punch a few holes in the pouch so that when it heats the aromas of the wood chips will emerge to flavour your food.

Smoke the Chips: Start the chips smoking by placing the pouch in the barbecue over high heat. Once smoke has started seeping from the wood chips in the smoking pouch, turn the heat down to low-medium (within a range of 200 to 300° F [95 to 150° C]). Let the chips smoke by themselves for 10 minutes, which allows any bitter impurities in the wood to be burned off.

Place your food on the burner that has no heat for the time indicated in the recipes.

Direct versus Indirect Cooking

In the direct method of cooking on the barbecue, you use smoke and heat from the burners underneath to cook your food. Use this method for chicken, fully cooked sausages, fully cooked ham and the like.

In the indirect method of cooking, the food being cooked is not on the burner with the heat—away from the heat source, it cooks just from the radiant heat enclosed in the barbecue, like an oven. Use this method for chorizo, andouille sausage, smoked salmon and so on.

Cast Iron Skillet Cooking

I discovered this method when I ran out of space on my cooktop in my kitchen. I put my cast iron frying pan right on the burner, heated it to smoking hot, and threw some potatoes into it. The key is to heat the pan until it is almost white hot.

Cedar Plank Cooking

This method of cooking originates on the West Coast. You will need small planks of *untreated* cedar. Do not use treated or recycled cedar.

You'll need a bucket of water handy near the barbecue to douse the flames if the board seriously catches on fire, and a sprayer filled with water to douse minor flames. It doesn't matter if the board burns a little; you don't re-use it.

Skewers

You can cook skewered chunks of meat, vegetables, fruit, fish and seafood on the barbecue. Metal skewers are better than bamboo, which need to be soaked in water for about 30 minutes before threading the chunks of food on them. Make sure you space out the chunks so they cook properly.

Barbecue Flavours

Marinades

There is a misconception that marinades will tenderize meats. They will not, but what they will do is add moisture and flavour, which tricks us into believing the meat is tender.

Remember not to over-marinate—marinating for too long can cause the meat to become excessively salty or, in the case of a high-acid marinade, may start to actually "cook" it.

Brines

Brines are a great way to add flavour and moisture to leaner cuts. They are basically salt and sugar solutions with water. The science behind it is quite detailed, but the short story is that the brine allows the meat to absorb the water and any flavourings in the brine. When the meat is grilled or barbecued, the cells in the meat retain that moisture and flavour and don't dry out, leaving the meat more flavourful.

One key step to brining is to make sure you rinse the meat well after you take it out of the brine and before barbecuing it.

Rubs

Rubs are basically mixtures of different spices that are "rubbed" into the meat before barbecuing. Rubs can take on many different flavours and even textures, from being very fine and almost delicate, to coarse and rough.

Instead of purchasing commercially prepared rubs, make your own. They are very easy to make and you can adapt them to different meats and foods that you are cooking. That way you will develop your own unique barbecue flavour.

Barbecue Sauces

Barbecue sauces not only add flavour to the item being barbecued, but they also help to keep it moist. Sauces are probably the most unique aspect of barbecuing and the easiest way to personalize your barbecue repertoire. They can range all the way from a tangy tomato-based sauce to a salty soy-based sauce.

Remember that because of their high sugar content, you must apply them at the very end of cooking.

Meats

Barbecuing and grilling are really simple methods of cooking foods, and because of that, try to use the best quality, freshest ingredients you can find. Go to your local farmers' market, whether it be Granville Island in Vancouver, the St. Lawrence market in Toronto, or the market in Millarville, Alberta—find out from the farmers what the best of the season is.

I come from Alberta, where beef is king, but Manitoba bison, Muscovy duck from Quebec and Salt Spring Island lamb are only a sampling of the regional delicacies that this country has to offer—all we have to do is search.

Meat and wild game products are available locally in most places in Canada. For example, sausages—German, Ukrainian, Italian, Polish, you name it—are being made all over the country.

Fish and Seafood

Fish and seafood are readily available fresh and frozen from supermarkets and specialty fish stores. If you can, use Digby scallops from Nova Scotia (they're better than scallops from elsewhere because they have lower water content), East Coast lobster, and British

Columbia salmon and halibut. Plenty of different local fish, including goldeye, whitefish, perch and pickerel could be substituted for any of the fish recipes here.

Vegetables

Grow your own vegetables in your garden, or get them fresh and local at farmers' markets, U-pick gardens and the like. Asparagus from Edgar Farms in Innisfail, Alberta, is worth seeking out. Portobellos are the big, meaty mushroom caps that are actually large button mushrooms. Yukon Gold potatoes were developed at the University of Guelph in the 1960s and are now a favourite among chefs worldwide.

Sauces

Sauces served with a dish can ramp up the flavour of a variety of meats, vegetables and salads. For example, my Grapefruit Drizzle Sauce, p. 72, goes well with any poultry. Horseradish Crème Frâiche, p. 82, and Mango Chutney Peppercorn Sauce, p. 106, pair really well with beef, and Wild Blueberry Sauce, p. 110, goes great with game meats.

Strawberry Salsa, p. 120, is a great topping for any grilled meat or fish, and Roasted Tomato Salsa, p. 124, is a beautiful all-purpose salsa that's good on anything.

Roasted Garlic Aioli, p. 12, and Bagna Cadu, p. 132, are great dipping sauces for veggie trays, breads, potatoes, you name it. Basil Mayonnaise, p. 116, is terrific on burgers and in sandwiches. Green Pea Guacamole, p. 130, is my take on the traditional guacamole with avocadoes, but you can just go out to your garden to get the ingredients.

Butters

I love butter; it has such a great flavour. You can add herbs, honey, maple syrup and even Grandma's raspberry jam, whip it together with the butter, wrap it in plastic and freeze it until you're ready to use it. Just a little dollop on top of grilled meats takes your grilling to the next level.

Dressings and Vinaigrettes

One of the basic sauces, vinaigrettes are oil and vinegars blended together with seasonings. Once again, take what is local and in your area. The Okanagan and Niagara valleys produce not only great grapes but wonderful fruit juices and honeys that can be incorporated into vinaigrettes. It is a great way to add flavours to your dish very easily.

There are three variations of honey vinaigrette here (pp. 38, 52 and 102). Other dressings and vinaigrettes are Ranch Dressing, p. 48—great with potatoes but also good with spicy drumsticks—Sun-dried Tomato Dressing, p. 50, Feta and Pepper Relish, p. 68 and Pomegranate Vinaigrette, p. 128. Try these on salads and on grilled meats for some flavour variations.

Five Simple Steps to Success

When the warm weather is finally here, we are able to enjoy the Canadian summer, which for me means lots of barbecuing. I have come up with five simple steps to help make every cookout a great success.

1. Control the heat: Start your barbecue on high, then turn the heat down to medium or medium-high.

This method will allow you to cook the inside of your food without burning the outside.

2. Blot the meat: Before putting anything on the barbecue, try to rid the surface of any moisture. Use a paper towel or clean dish towel to blot the meat on all sides.

Moisture on the surface will cause the food to steam instead of grill.

3. Season properly: Put a little extra salt or seasoning on the food; some will fall off during the cooking process.

4. Clean the grill frequently: A good wire brush and a wipe with a rag soaked in oil helps to keep the grill non-stick every time you use it.

Clean the grill before you cook (after it's preheated) and after you take the food off the grill.

5. Sauce in the last five minutes: Most sauces contain a lot of sugar and or oil, so apply the sauce in the very last minutes of cooking.

Barbecuing and grilling are like golf: you need to practise to hone your skills.

About this Book

This book is written by a Canadian chef, born and raised. The recipes and methods are quite simple, and they should be used as guidelines. Write notes, add your own ingredients, modify to your family's likes and dislikes. The home chefs are truly the best chefs, because they know how to cook for their families.

Because all barbecues are a little different, take a little extra care and attention when dealing with cooking times the first time that you try a recipe, especially considering the weather here in Canada.

The book starts with some Tapas from the Grill to keep you and your friends and family occupied while the rest of the food cooks. The next section includes dishes cooked on the side burner or main grill. There's some cast iron skillet recipes, and some salads and a cedar-plank dish.

Big Fires is the biggest section of the book, dealing with grilling a wide variety of meats, fish and seafood. I've included the barbecue sauces and so on here, because this is where they're used. The Smoking Hot section unravels the mysteries of using a barbecue as a smoker to create great flavours.

Finally, the Fire's Out section contains desserts for when the barbecue is cooling off. A handful of favourite grilling recipes from the Company's Coming Test Kitchen have also been spinkled throughout the book.

One last tidbit is that barbecuing and grilling go much better with a cold beer or great glass of Canadian wine in your hand. Microbreweries have sprung up nearly everywhere, and we make great wine from Vancouver Island to New Brunswick, Niagara and Okanagan. Make sure you buy these products and support the producers.

Grilled Calamari with Chickpeas

Serves 4 to 6 as an appetizer

When we think of calamari in restaurants across the country, we think of deep-fried, rubbery blobs that are usually greasy and somewhat tasteless. Because the calamari in this recipe is grilled quickly, it stays tender and tasty. It also picks up a hint of smokiness from the barbecue. The chickpeas add a nice lemony contrast to the squid.

2 lbs (1 kg) squid tubes

2¼ cups (560 mL) olive oil

juice and zest from 1 lemon

¼ tsp (1 mL) crushed red chili flakes

½ tsp (2 mL) ground cumin

¼ cup (60 mL) chopped fresh parsley

½ cup (125 mL) sliced red onion

1 x 19 oz (540 g) can chickpeas

Wash and rinse squid very well, including the inside of the tubes. Pat dry and place in a large bowl. In a smaller bowl, mix together oil, lemon juice, zest and chili flakes. Pour half of this mixture over the squid. Coat well and refrigerate for 1 hour.

In a large bowl, add the remaining oil mixture and cumin, parsley, red onions and chickpeas. Adjust for seasoning, and set aside.

Preheat the barbecue to hot. Grill calamari for 2 to 3 minutes per side, or until flesh turns opaque.

To serve, mound chickpea mixture in the middle of a platter and top with calamari.

Tip

When you buy the squid for this recipe, choose smaller tubes: smaller calamari is more tender.

🌿 *This recipe is a great source of protein; it's also a tasty, low-calorie appetizer.*

Skewered Yukon Gold Potatoes with Roasted Garlic Aioli

Serves 4 to 6

Potatoes are usually a starch served with a meal, not an appetizer. These skewered potatoes make tasty little snacks before the main course—you can eat them right off the skewer like you're eating a corn dog on the midway at the local summer fair. The potatoes are great cold as a snack, and they can be served with any grilled meat or fish. I like Yukon Gold potatoes—developed in the 1960s at the University of Guelph, they have a tasty, golden flesh—but you can use any variety of baby potatoes you can find at the market.

Roasted Garlic

1 head garlic

1 Tbsp (15 mL) olive oil

salt and pepper

Roasted Garlic Aioli

1 cup (250 mL) mayonnaise (not salad dressing)

1 head garlic, roasted and mashed

1 Tbsp (15 mL) chopped fresh parsley

1 Tbsp (15 mL) freshly squeezed lemon juice

2 lbs (1 kg) baby potatoes

6 to 8 skewers (see Tip)

1/4 cup (60 mL) olive oil

1 tsp (5 mL) paprika

1 Tbsp (15 mL) tomato paste

1 Tbsp (15 mL) sherry vinegar

salt and pepper

For the roasted garlic, preheat the barbecue to medium-high. Slice the top 1/2 inch (1 cm) off the stem end of the head of garlic. Drizzle with olive oil and season with salt and pepper. Wrap in foil and grill for 1 hour or until golden and soft. When cool enough to handle, simply squeeze out the garlic cloves and mash.

To make the aioli, blend all ingredients together in a small bowl and refrigerate until needed.

Parboil whole baby potatoes for 7 minutes. Drain and chill until needed.

Preheat the barbecue to medium-high. Mix olive oil, paprika, tomato paste and sherry vinegar together in a large bowl. Season to taste with salt and pepper. Add parboiled potatoes and toss to ensure even coating. Skewer potatoes and grill for 15 to 20 minutes, flipping frequently. To serve, pull potatoes off skewers and dip into garlic aioli.

Tip

You can roast the garlic ahead of time and refrigerate it until ready to use.

Tip

If you are using bamboo skewers, soak them in water for a couple of hours before they hit the grill.

Traditional aioli is made with raw egg blended with olive oil and garlic. As a result of possible health concerns with raw eggs, we use mayonnaise in this recipe.

Blue Cheese and Almond-stuffed Dates Wrapped with Pancetta

Makes about 40

These tidbits are absolutely the best. I cannot emphasize enough that you should try, try, try them, especially with a great bottle of red wine. The sweetness of the dates, the richness of the cheese and the saltiness of the pancetta combine to make a great treat. I like to cook the dates right on the grill, but you could also put them on a foil baking dish and bake them in your barbecue.

1 x 2 lb (1 kg) box of dates

½ lb (250 g) blue cheese or goat cheese

40 almonds

30 thin slices pancetta (see Tip)

Preheat the barbecue to medium.

If the dates have pits, you must first remove all the pits. Do all of them; it will make your life a lot easier. Stuff each date with ½ to 1 tsp (2 to 5 mL) cheese and an almond. Close the date around the cheese and the almond, trying to make sure that all of the cheese stays in the date.

Take each round slice of pancetta and cut it in half. Wrap a half-slice around each date, making sure that it goes around all the way.

Grill for 2 to 3 minutes per side, or until crispy and cheese begins to melt. Serve at once.

Tip

Pancetta is Italian bacon. It comes in a cylinder shape in the deli section of most grocery stores across the country. Ask the deli staff to cut the pancetta into thin slices for this recipe.

Bourbon Chicken Wings

Makes 30 to 35 wings

A can't-miss, sure-to-please recipe from the Company's Coming collection. Add dimension to your favourite barbecue sauce with the heady richness of bourbon and the satisfying sweetness of orange juice and honey. Guests will happily hover around—and quickly devour—a basket of these tasty wings.

3 lbs (1.5 kg) split chicken wings, tips discarded

Bourbon Barbecue Sauce

1 cup (250 mL) barbecue sauce

$\frac{1}{2}$ cup (125 mL) bourbon

$\frac{1}{4}$ cup (60 mL) frozen concentrated orange juice

$\frac{1}{4}$ cup (60 mL) liquid honey

1 tsp (5 mL) seasoned salt

Combine Bourbon Barbecue Sauce ingredients, reserving $\frac{1}{2}$ cup (125 mL).

Pour remaining barbecue sauce mixture into a large resealable freezer bag. Add chicken wings and chill for 2 hours. Drain and discard marinade. Grill wings on direct medium-low heat for about 15 minutes per side until no longer pink at the bone. Brush with reserved barbecue sauce mixture during final 10 minutes of cooking.

Tip
Try different shades of flavour by using a smoky barbecue sauce one time and a hot and spicy one the next.

Tip

Pile the wings high on a plate or in a parchment paper–lined basket. Have finger bowls with water and a slice of orange at the ready.

Prosciutto Pork Mignon with Parsley Cilantro Crema

Serves 6

Jean Paré's Golden Rule of Cooking is to "never share a recipe you wouldn't use yourself." You'll be sharing this favourite from the Company's Coming library many times over! Ribbons of prosciutto wrap superbly seasoned slices of tenderloin. The tangy sauce adds vibrancy to both the plate and the palate.

2 x 1 lb (500 g) pork tenderloins, ends trimmed

Rub
1½ tsp (7 mL) ground cumin

1½ tsp (7 mL) ground coriander

1½ tsp (7 mL) chili powder

½ tsp (2 mL) sugar

salt and pepper

Parsley Cilantro Crema
1 cup (250 mL) fresh flat-leaf parsley

½ cup (125 mL) fresh cilantro

¼ cup (60 mL) olive oil

3 Tbsp (45 mL) lime juice

2 cloves garlic, minced

1 tsp (5 mL) sugar

1 tsp (5 mL) ground cumin

salt and pepper

½ cup (125 mL) sour cream

12 prosciutto slices

4 double-pronged skewers

In a blender or food processor, process all Parsley Cilantro Crema ingredients except sour cream until smooth. Add sour cream and process until just combined. Serve at room temperature.

Cut tenderloins crosswise into 6 slices each, about 1½ inches (4 cm) thick. Combine rub ingredients and rub on pork slices.

Fold prosciutto slices in half lengthwise and wrap 1 slice around each pork slice, overlapping if necessary. Thread pork onto skewers, leaving a 1 inch (2.5 cm) space between portions. Grill on direct medium-high heat for 5 to 6 minutes per side until internal temperature reaches 160° F (71° C). Serve with Parsley Cilantro Crema.

Tip
Fresh flat-leaf parsley leaves make an excellent garnish for this dish.

Although there are many species of parsley, two are most commonly used in cooking. Flat-leaf parsley is preferable for cooking because of its stronger, fresher flavour and its higher tolerance for heat, while the more common curly-leafed parsley has a mild flavour that makes it more suitable as a garnish.

Grilled Sourdough Bread

Serves 4 to 6

Sourdough bread begins as a yeasty, tangy blob of starter that was essential in the survival of prospectors working the gold fields in British Columbia and the Yukon more than a century ago. I just love the crunchiness of this bread, with a great olive oil or flavoured butter (pp. 32, 42), or use the pieces of bread as rafts for salads, steak, whatever you like on top. The bread is infused with the delicious taste of raw garlic. You can use the method here for any kind of bread—pita, baguette, Naan bread, etc.

1 day-old loaf sourdough bread

½ cup (125 mL) extra-virgin olive oil

1 head garlic, cloves separated and peeled but left whole

Preheat the barbecue to high. Cut bread into ½-inch (1 cm) slices, and brush liberally on both sides with oil. In small batches of 6 to 8 pieces, grill bread for about 2 minutes a side, flipping once, or until golden brown. Some charred bits are fine.

Remove from grill and rub a garlic clove against each slice of bread, almost as if you were grating cheese. Serve bread immediately with a small bowl of olive oil for dipping, or a flavoured butter of your choice.

CW *Instead of buying those hard, crunchy croutons they sell in stores, make your own croutons out of leftover slices of this bread. Terrific on any salad!*

Cast Iron Potatoes

Serves 6 to 8

One day I ran out of space on my cook top, so I decided to cook the potatoes in my cast iron skillet right on the grill. It turned out to be one of the easiest recipes ever—and the bonus is that you can cook something else on the other side of the barbecue while the potatoes are cooking. The smoke from whatever you cook on the other grill will add more flavour to the potatoes. I use extra-virgin canola oil, which gives a very earthy, fragrant taste to the potatoes, *and* it's good for you.

2 to 3 lbs (1 to 1.5 kg) baby potatoes, any variety, unpeeled

water

2 Tbsp (30 mL) extra-virgin canola oil or extra-virgin olive oil

1 Tbsp (15 mL) roughly chopped fresh thyme (or your favourite fresh herb)

salt and pepper

Preheat the barbecue to high. Wash potatoes well, then place in cast iron pan. Pour enough water in pan to just cover the potatoes. Place pan on the grill and close the lid of the barbecue.

Check doneness in 30 minutes; most of the water should have boiled away. If it hasn't, keep cooking until all the water is gone. Continue to cook the potatoes in the pan, rolling them around so that their skins get crispy and just begin to break. At this point, drizzle with the oil and fresh herbs, and season with salt and pepper.

Canola is a Canadian invention developed in the 1970s. A member of the cabbage family, canola produces an oil that has a fatty acid profile similar to that of extra-virgin olive oil, with lots of healthy omega-3 and omega-6.

Caramelized Cast Iron Scallops with Drambuie Butter

Serves 8 to 10 as an appetizer

This recipe is perfect for that side burner on your barbecue, or one of those Bunsen burners. It's a great appetizer at a more formal event, or for Canada Day—what could be more perfect than Digby scallops from the East Coast? These scallops are quite large, which is what you want for this recipe. The numbers "10/20" mean that there are roughly 10 to 20 per pound.

2 lbs (1 kg) 10/20 scallops

2 Tbsp (30 mL) canola oil

¼ cup (60 mL) butter

1 Tbsp (15 mL) Drambuie or Scotch

1 Tbsp (15 mL) maple syrup

salt and pepper

The first thing you want to do here is heat your cast iron skillet on the side burner or grill—it will need a good 10 to 15 minutes to get white hot. While the skillet is getting hot, dry the scallops well so that there is no moisture on them.

Next, place the canola oil on a plate and dip both flat surfaces of each scallop in the oil, making sure to cover each one evenly. Do all of the scallops at one time even though you will be cooking them in small batches. Place the first batch of scallops flat-side down in the hot skillet, and gently push on them until they are flat against the pan. Cook for 2 to 3 minutes, just until the one side is caramelized.

Flip and cook the other side for 1 minute, until the scallops are just done. Remove to a warm plate, and put the next batch of pre-oiled scallops into the skillet.

Once scallops are cooked, add butter, Drambuie (or Scotch) and maple syrup to the pan and stir until butter has melted. Season to taste with salt and pepper. Remove the pan from heat (it will still be quite hot), and put the scallops back into the pan just to coat with the sauce. Serve immediately.

Most scallops in Canada are from the clean, cold waters near Digby, Nova Scotia. Canadian scallops have a lower water content than those from the U.S. Our scallops are much better—the difference is like night and day.

Cast Iron Mussels

Serves 4 to 6

Keeping foods simple, I think, is one of the best ways to let the flavour of the food come out. In this dish, the taste of the mussels really comes out because they are not immersed in a broth. As the mussels start to cook, their juices hit the pan and infuse them with the smokiness of their own sizzling hot liquid. All this recipe needs is some bread and a great white wine.

3 lbs (1.5 kg) mussels, cleaned and de-bearded (see Tip)

¼ cup (60 mL) olive oil

1 Tbsp (15 mL) crushed garlic

2 Tbsp (30 mL) chopped chives

salt and pepper

your choice of bread

Heat a cast iron pan on the side burner or grill over high heat for 15 minutes—the pan has to be absolutely scorching hot. Dump the mussels into the pan. While they are cooking, mix together oil, garlic and chives in a small bowl. Once the mussels have steamed open, pour the oil mixture over the mussels, and season with salt and pepper. Serve with a loaf of your favourite bread.

Tip

To de-beard the mussels, grasp the stringy bits using a dishcloth and pull them gently off.

The Ordre de Bon Temps, founded by Samuel de Champlain at Port-Royal in 1606, was formed to raise the spirits of early French settlers. One item featured in this first Canadian dinner club was mussels cooked on a board with pine needles providing the flavouring.

Butter-basted Rib-eye Steak

Serves 2 to 4

This is steak you only want to have once in a while—it's a cardiologist's favourite steak. It is rich, meaty and well caramelized on the outside—and it melts in your mouth. As with the other cast iron pan recipes here, the key is to get the pan scorching hot. Season the meat well and do not overcook it—anything past medium may be too much.

2 lbs (1 kg) thick rib-eye or prime rib steak

1 Tbsp (15 mL) canola oil

1 Tbsp (15 mL) kosher salt

¼ cup (60 mL) cold butter

1 Tbsp (15 mL) cracked black pepper

Rub the meat with oil and generously season with kosher salt on all sides. If the meat has been refrigerated, allow it to come to room temperature.

Heat a cast iron skillet on the side burner or grill for about 15 minutes until very hot. Place steak in the hot pan; there should be lots of smoke. Press steak down to make sure that the surface makes contact with the pan. Cook for 7 to 10 minutes depending on the thickness of the meat. Flip, add butter to the pan and baste the steak, cooking for 5 minutes. Turn heat to low and cook for another 5 minutes, or until it reaches desired doneness (remember, not past medium). Meanwhile, continue to baste with the butter and season with pepper.

Tip

An instant-read thermometer takes the guesswork out of doneness in this recipe.

Southern Alberta is cattle country. The industry began in the 1870s with the arrival of the Mounties. Chinook winds and plentiful sheltered valleys and streams created the ideal environment for raising cattle.

Mushroom Ragout

Serves 4 to 6 as a side

You can use any mushrooms in this recipe: oyster, chanterelles, shiitake, brown, button, etc. If you can get fresh wild mushrooms for this recipe, that's great, but button mushrooms from any grocery will work as well. Sometimes grocery stores will stock wild mushrooms, or you can check out the local farmers' markets. Morels usually appear in markets in spring, and throughout the summer different varieties are available across the country.

2 Tbsp (30 mL) extra-virgin olive oil

1 tsp (5 mL) or more crushed red chili flakes

3 or more cloves garlic, peeled but whole

½ onion, sliced

2 lbs (1 kg) mushrooms

½ cup (125 mL) white wine

4 tomatoes, diced

2 Tbsp (30 mL) balsamic vinegar

2 Tbsp (30 mL) chopped fresh herbs (oregano, thyme, rosemary or a combination)

In a large skillet or Dutch oven pot on grill or side burner, gently heat olive oil over medium heat. Add red chili flakes and, when they begin to crackle and cook, add garlic. Cook until golden brown, then toss in the onion and cook for 3 to 5 minutes or until soft. Add all of the mushrooms and cook for 3 to 5 minutes. Put remaining ingredients in the pot and turn heat to medium-low. Gently simmer, stirring occasionally, for up to 45 minutes.

There may be a lot of liquid at the beginning—it's just the mushrooms releasing their water. When most of the liquid has been reduced, taste and adjust the seasonings.

Serve right from the cooking vessel with any grilled meat.

Tip

If you're out in the backwoods of Canada picking mushrooms yourself, make sure you have an authoritative identification guide: some species are poisonous.

For a delicious mushroom bruschetta appetizer, roughly chop the mushrooms before cooking as per the recipe, and put on toasted Italian bread slices.

Cedar-planked Arctic Char with Maple Compound Butter

Serves 4 to 6

The tantalizing, cedary smell of this recipe cooking on the barbecue will drive your neighbours crazy. There is no need to soak the cedar boards—doing so will actually leech out a lot of the flavour. Make sure that you have a pail of water nearby for after you are finished with the planks; you'll need the water to put out the smoldering pieces of wood. Also, make sure you use untreated raw cedar. A chef friend of mine near Sechelt on the Sunshine Coast of British Columbia used recycled, treated cedar siding for his version of this recipe—it's lucky no one died.

2 untreated, rough cedar planks 1 foot (30 cm) long

1 x 8 oz (250 g) fillet arctic char per person

salt and pepper

Maple Compound Butter

½ lb (250 g) butter

¼ cup (60 mL) pure maple syrup

1 Tbsp (15 mL) chopped fresh thyme

1 Tbsp (15 mL) fresh lemon juice

salt and pepper

For the maple compound butter, whip butter in a stand mixer until fluffy and pale. Mix the other ingredients together in a separate bowl and slowly add to butter. Continue to whip until butter is well combined. Dollop onto plastic wrap, roll up into a cylinder with the ends of the wrap twisted, and refrigerate.

Preheat the barbecue to medium to medium-high and have a mister or pitcher of water standing by (in addition to the pail of water). Put the planks right on the barbecue and then put the fillets on the planks. Close the lid of the barbecue.

After 10 minutes, raise the lid to see how the fish is doing. The planks should be smoking and may even be burning. If they are, douse flames with a little water. It is okay for the boards to burn a little. Close the lid and check frequently for about 5 to 10 minutes more until done. Season with salt and pepper, and serve topped with a thin slice of Maple Compound Butter.

Do not save the board to use again in this recipe.

Tip

Cylinders of flavoured butter may be frozen. If you want to get fancy, pipe rosettes of butter onto a wax paper–covered baking sheet and freeze. When frozen, rosettes can be stored in a sealable plastic bag until needed.

Cooking fish this way is a method based on traditional native cooking on the West Coast, where salmon and cedar were both plentiful.

This recipe is a real coast-to-coast-to-coast Canadian treat—arctic char from the North, maple syrup from the East and cedar from the West Coast.

Confit-style Salmon

Serves 4

Traditional confits involve cooking meat such as duck in fat, but this recipe just infuses the salmon with a great flavour that it acquires by marinating in the fridge overnight. You can cook the salmon right on the grill or in a cast iron skillet. Wild salmon from Campbell River, on Vancouver Island, is the best in this recipe.

4 x 8 oz (250 g) salmon fillets or steaks

2 cups (500 mL) extra-virgin olive oil

2 Tbsp (30 mL) chopped fresh basil

2 Tbsp (30 mL) chopped fresh parsley

2 Tbsp (30 mL) chopped fresh oregano

salt and pepper

freshly squeezed lemon juice

lemon wedges

Mix oil and herbs together in a medium bowl and season with salt and pepper. Place salmon in a baking dish and pour olive oil–herb mixture over the fish, flipping to coat both sides of the fish. Cover and refrigerate overnight.

Preheat the barbecue to medium-high and grease the grills well. Remove the fish from the olive oil and herb mixture; wipe as much oil from the salmon as possible. Grill fish, flesh-side down first, for 5 minutes per inch (2.5 cm) of thickness, or until desired doneness. Flip fish partway through.

To serve, squeeze lemon juice on the salmon and garnish with lemon wedges.

Cast Iron Method

Heat a cast iron skillet over high heat until wisp of smoke just curls up from the pan. Place fish flesh-side down, and cook for 5 minutes. Flip and cook an additional 5 minutes, or until desired doneness. Serve as described above.

Cajun-crusted Chicken Quesadillas with Roasted Apples and Cheese

Serves 4 to 6

This great recipe will take care of the abundance of apples from your backyard tree.

Part A

1 lb (500 g) boneless, skinless chicken breasts

¼ cup (60 mL) Cajun spice or Barbecue Rub (p. 56)

Part B

4 apples, peeled, cored and sliced

½ cup (125 mL) brown sugar

Part C

2 cups (500 mL) shredded cheese (use Cheddar, Tex-Mex or your favourite artisanal cheese)

Part D

12 x 10-inch (30 x 25 cm) flour tortillas (flavoured or unflavoured)

Preheat the barbecue to medium-high. Put the Cajun spice into a sealable plastic bag and toss each chicken breast, one at a time, as if you were making Shake and Bake. Make sure that the chicken is well coated—it may seem like a lot of spice, but it all comes together in the end.

Grill chicken for 5 to 7 minutes per side or until cooked, then slice against the grain into ¼-inch (0.5 cm) slices and set aside.

Preheat the barbecue to medium. Toss the apple slices in brown sugar to coat well. Place in a foil lasagna pan and bake in the barbecue with the lid closed for 10 to 15 minutes, stirring every 5 minutes. Remove from barbecue and cool to room temperature.

To assemble the quesadillas, lay out 6 flat tortillas and the chicken slices, apples and cheese. Start by filling the bottom half of each tortilla with a thin layer of chicken, followed by the apples, followed by the cheese. Once all 6 have been filled, fold over the unfilled tortilla halves to make half-moon shaped quesadillas. Repeat with the second batch of 6 tortillas.

Grill over medium heat for approximately 3 to 5 minutes per side, rotating half a turn once to ensure nice grill marks. Allow the quesadillas to sit for 2 minutes. Cut each quesadilla into quarters and pile on a platter. Serve with salsas, hot peppers, Green Pea Guacamole (p. 130), or whatever condiments you like.

Artisanal cheesemakers across the country are becoming known worldwide for the quality of their goat's milk cheeses. In addition to chèvre, you will find feta, Brie and Gouda at farmers' markets.

Grilled Asparagus with Honey Vinaigrette, Feta and Bee Pollen

Serves 4 to 6

Asparagus, honey and feta make a great combination on their own, so if you can't find bee pollen, don't worry—the recipe will be just fine without it. I like the asparagus grown by Edgar Farms, in Innisfail, Alberta, but use whatever you can find at the market. You can probably find wildflower honey there as well. Also, try other cheeses if you like. This dish is best served at room temperature, which is perfect for a large crowd or for a brunch.

1 lb (500 g) fresh asparagus

2 tsp (10 mL) canola oil

salt and pepper

Honey Vinaigrette

1 Tbsp (15 mL) Dijon mustard

2 Tbsp (30 mL) honey (wildflower honey is my favourite)

2 Tbsp (30 mL) red wine vinegar, or any vinegar other than plain white

½ cup (125 mL) extra-virgin olive oil

1 to 2 garlic cloves, peeled but left whole (optional)

salt and pepper

½ cup (125 mL) crumbled feta cheese

1 Tbsp (15 mL) bee pollen

Preheat the barbecue to medium-high. Wash asparagus well, and pat dry. Toss the asparagus with canola oil to coat each piece thoroughly. Grill asparagus for roughly 5 minutes, or until tender. Watch them carefully, as they may flare up—a little charred is okay, a lot charred is not! Season asparagus with salt and pepper and place on a platter. Set aside while you make the vinaigrette.

Place vinaigrette ingredients in a small glass jar. Cover and shake well. Taste the dressing to ensure that the seasoning is correct and balanced. Do not be afraid to adjust to your liking.

To serve, drizzle ¼ cup (60 mL) vinaigrette over the asparagus, top with feta cheese, then sprinkle with bee pollen.

Tip

The whole garlic in this recipe just adds flavour to the dressing—you don't actually eat it.

Tip

An uber-Canadian variation on this recipe is to use fiddlehead greens instead of asparagus. They're the early-spring fronds of a type of fern collected in the wilds of the back country, and they're available for a very short time in June. Watch carefully for their arrival.

Grilled Vegetable Salad

Serves 4 to 6

This great salad can be served at room temperature, or hot or cold. It doesn't matter what vegetables you use—check out your garden or the market and see what's available. You can pile it on rafts of Grilled Sourdough Bread (p. 20) or throw some fried or poached eggs on top with some toast, and you have a great brunch item.

2 portobello mushrooms, sliced ½ inch (1 cm) thick

4 Tbsp (60 mL) olive oil, *divided*

salt and pepper

2 zucchini, sliced ½ inch (1 cm) thick

1 lb (500 g) onion, sliced ½ inch (1 cm) thick

3 peppers (mixed colours), quartered, seeded and stem removed

2 Tbsp (30 mL) balsamic vinegar

fresh herbs

Preheat the barbecue to medium-high. In a large bowl, toss mushrooms with 1 Tbsp (30 mL) oil, and season with salt and pepper. Repeat with the rest of the vegetables. Grill until browned, about 3 to 5 minutes, flipping once or twice.

Place the balsamic vinegar in a large bowl. Remove vegetables from barbecue, and toss them with the balsamic in the bowl. Season to taste with salt, pepper and fresh herbs.

Serve warm, room temperature or cold.

Tip

Leftovers are great tossed with pasta.

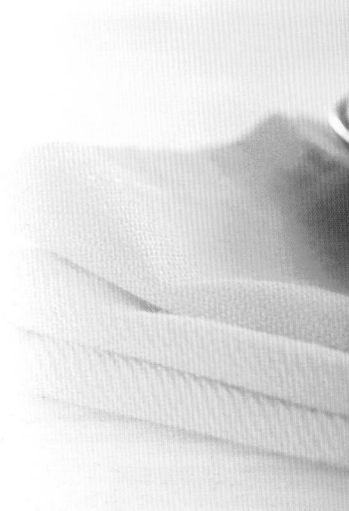

Corn with More Than Just Butter

Serves 6

I think every province celebrates summer with corn. In Alberta, Taber corn is sold from roadside stands from late July into September. Just the thought of Peaches and Cream or Krispy King gets everybody's mouths watering. I like to remove the husk and get grill marks right on the kernels. The corn picks up the smoky flavour, and some kernels get caramelized. Serve the corn with some of the butters provided below.

6 ears of corn, husks removed

1 Tbsp (15 mL) canola oil

Place corn and canola oil in a medium bowl and mix well to combine.

Preheat the barbecue to high. Brush corn with oil and grill for 15 to 20 minutes, flipping frequently, until golden brown and the sugars in the corn are caramelized.

For each of the butters, place all ingredients in a medium bowl and mix well to combine. You want the butters to have maximum spreadibility when you are serving them with corn, so make sure they are at room temperature.

Chipotle Lime Butter

4 oz (125 g) butter, room temperature

1 Tbsp (15 mL) chopped, canned chipotle (or to taste)

1 tsp (5 mL) freshly squeezed lime juice

salt and pepper to taste

Honey Thyme Butter

4 oz (125 g) butter, room temperature

1 Tbsp (15 mL) honey

1 tsp (5 mL) chopped fresh thyme

salt and pepper to taste

Gorgonzola Butter

4 oz (125 g) butter, room temperature

2 Tbsp (30 mL) Gorgonzola cheese, room temperature

salt and pepper to taste

Corn is native to the Americas and was an important crop among the earliest peoples. Today, sweet corn grows in areas with hot summer days and cool nights—anywhere from BC's Fraser and Okanagan valleys to the Maritimes.

Grilled Perogies

Serves 6 to 8 as an appetizer

I grew up on perogies—they're still one of the best foods ever invented. If you don't make your own, try to buy some from a church or local community centre—handmade perogies have much better flavour than store-bought ones. This recipe is a great snack while waiting for the main barbecue event. The perogies are crisp on the outside and creamy and rich on the inside.

3 dozen perogies, any filling, cooked and chilled (see Tip)

2 Tbsp (30 mL) canola oil

salt and pepper

Preheat the barbecue to medium-high heat. Brush or toss cold perogies with canola oil until very well coated. Grill perogies for about 5 minutes per side, or until light golden brown. The filling might start to ooze out if the perogies get too hot.

Take perogies off grill and season with salt and pepper. I like to serve them with Roasted Tomato Salsa (p. 124) and Ranch Dressing (p. 48).

Tip

The secret to this dish is to cook the perogies first, then chill them until you're ready to barbecue them. To cook perogies, place them in a pot of salted, boiling water until they float to the surface.

Romano Ciabatta Vegetable Salad

Serves 6

The smoky sweetness of grilled vegetables is enhanced by a roasted garlic and balsamic vinaigrette. This salad, a Company's Coming favourite, is a tasty vegetarian meal that everyone at the table will enjoy.

2 large fennel bulbs (white part only), cut into 4 wedges each (see Tip)

1 large red onion, cut into 4 wedges (see Tip)

1 large eggplant, cut into ¾ inch (2 cm) slices

2 medium zucchini, quartered lengthwise

1 large red pepper, halved

1 large yellow pepper, halved

¼ cup (60 mL) extra-virgin olive oil

2 multigrain ciabatta buns, split

1 x 19 oz (540 mL) can of romano beans, rinsed and drained

2 cups (500 mL) grape tomatoes

Dressing

4 cloves roasted garlic, mashed (see Tip)

⅔ cup (150 mL) balsamic vinegar

⅔ cup (150 mL) extra-virgin olive oil

2 tsp (10 mL) sugar

salt and pepper

Preheat the barbecue to medium. Brush first 6 ingredients with olive oil. Grill fennel and onion for about 25 minutes, turning occasionally, until tender. Grill eggplant, zucchini and peppers for about 15 minutes, turning occasionally, until tender-crisp and browned. Let stand until cool enough to handle. Cut fennel and onion into 1 inch (2.5 cm) pieces. Cut eggplant, zucchini and peppers into 1½ inch (4 cm) pieces.

Brush bun halves with olive oil. Grill for 1 to 2 minutes until toasted. Cut into 1 inch (2.5 cm) pieces.

Combine beans and tomatoes with vegetables and bread cubes in a large bowl.

Combine dressing ingredients. Drizzle over salad and toss until coated. Makes about 12 cups (3 L).

Tip

Garnish with shaved Romano cheese and fresh oregano.

Tip

Quartering the onion with the stem still on helps the pieces stay intact during grilling. The core of the fennel serves the same stabilizing purpose.

Tip

To roast garlic, trim ¼ inch (6 mm) from each bulb to expose tops of cloves, leaving bulbs intact. Wrap bulbs individually in greased foil and bake at 350° F (175° C) for about 45 minutes until tender. Let stand until cool enough to handle. Squeeze garlic bulb to remove cloves from skins. Excess roasted garlic can be wrapped and stored in the freezer.

Potato Salad with Ranch Dressing

Serves 6 to 8

I think potatoes and ranch dressing go so well together in this easy recipe. You can use any kind of baby potatoes you like. I like creamers, reds or Yukon Golds for this recipe. Drizzle any leftover dressing on hot baked potatoes or serve as a dip with fresh garden vegetables. It is very important to toss the potatoes with the vinegar while they are still warm.

3 lbs (1.5 kg) baby potatoes

3 Tbsp (45 mL) cider vinegar

salt and pepper

¼ cup (60 mL) chopped green onions

2 Tbsp (30 mL) chopped fresh parsley

Ranch Dressing

1 cup (250 mL) mayonnaise (not salad dressing)

1 tsp (5 mL) granulated garlic or onion powder

2 tsp (10 mL) chopped chives or green onions, plus extra for garnish

2 tsp (10 mL) chopped parsley, plus extra for garnish

½ tsp (2 mL) garlic powder

½ tsp (2 mL) salt

½ tsp (2 mL) freshly ground black pepper

½ tsp (2 mL) dried oregano

½ tsp (2 mL) dried thyme

1½ cups (375 mL) buttermilk (regular or low fat)

Leave the skin on the potatoes and boil in a saucepan on your side burner or grill until fork tender, for about 25 minutes. Drain and set aside. When they are still warm but cool enough to handle, cut in half and toss with vinegar. Season with salt and pepper and chill.

Meanwhile, to make the dressing, blend together all ingredients in a bowl and set aside.

Once the potatoes are cold, toss with about 1 cup (250 mL) of dressing. Garnish with remaining chopped chives (or green onions) and parsley, and serve.

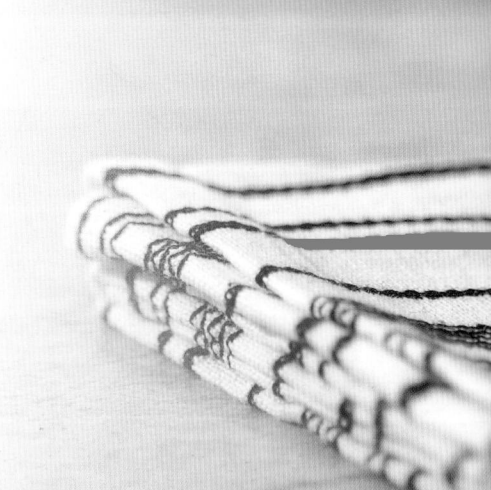

Prince Edward Island is famous for its bright red spuds, and if you can lay your hands on some of those, lucky you. Who hasn't heard of Stompin' Tom's Bud the Spud and "the bright red mud"?

Barley Salad with Sun-dried Tomato Dressing

Serves 6 to 8

Barley salad is a great alternative to a potato or pasta salad. The unique, nutty flavour of barley is just wonderful on a hot summer day, plus it's a grain product grown in our fine country (Canada is the second-largest barley producer in the world) *and* it's good for you. Buy pearl barley in small bags in the cereal aisle in the grocery store; it's different from pot barley, which is less refined. If you can get a variety of mixed mushrooms, try for crimini, button or field.

2 cups (500 mL) pearl barley

2 lbs (1 kg) mixed mushrooms

1 onion, thinly sliced

2 Tbsp (30 mL) canola oil

Sun-dried Tomato Dressing

¼ cup (60 mL) sun-dried tomatoes

½ cup (125 mL) hot water

½ cup (125 mL) canola oil

¼ cup (60 mL) red wine vinegar

2 Tbsp (30 mL) chopped fresh herbs (a variety of your favourites)

1 Tbsp (15 mL) flavoured mustard (any kind you like)

1 tsp (5 mL) honey

1 Tbsp (15 mL) balsamic vinegar

½ tsp (2mL) *each* salt and pepper

Cook barley according to package directions and set aside to cool.

In a pan on the side burner or grill, sauté mushrooms and onion over medium heat in the canola oil until light golden brown. Cool the mushroom mixture, then refrigerate.

While barley and mushrooms are cooking, re-hydrate the sun-dried tomatoes in hot water for 30 minutes. Drain, reserving ¼ cup (60 mL) of the water for the dressing. Set aside.

To make the dressing, roughly chop the sun-dried tomatoes and put them and the ¼ cup (60 mL) reserved water in a jar. Add remaining ingredients, cover and shake well. Adjust seasoning as necessary.

To assemble, toss mushroom mixture with barley and dressing in a large bowl. Serve at once.

Tip
The dressing can be stored in the fridge for 2 weeks.

Tip

Add whatever you like to this recipe—grilled peppers, squash, tomatoes—you name it.

Alberta Cobb Salad with Honey Vinaigrette

Serves 6 to 8

The great thing about this salad is that it looks great, 90 percent of the work can be done ahead of time to wow your guests, *and* it showcases some great local products. See what is available at the market—maybe fresh beets, baby carrots, baby sweet onions. I've suggested three types of common garden lettuce here, but use whatever you've got on hand. The point is to have a variety of greens.

½ head iceberg lettuce

½ head romaine lettuce

1 head butter leaf lettuce

2 tomatoes, diced

2 cups (500 mL) chopped chicken or leftover barbecued pork chops

1 cup (250 mL) cooked, crumbled bacon (8 slices)

4 hard-boiled eggs, peeled and sliced

1 cup (250 mL) crumbled blue cheese or your favourite cheese

1 cup (250 mL) blanched green peas (see Tip)

½ cup (125 mL) chopped chives or green onions

Wash lettuces well and tear into large pieces. Keep covered with a damp cloth—not wet! To assemble the salad, mix the lettuces together and line a large platter with them. Arrange the rest of the items in rows over top. Set aside while you make the dressing.

Place all vinaigrette ingredients in a jar, cover and shake well. Drizzle over salad and serve immediately.

Honey Vinaigrette

¼ cup (60 mL) red wine vinegar

1 tsp (5 mL) honey

juice from ½ lemon

1 tsp (5 mL) Worcestershire sauce

1 Tbsp (15 mL) Dijon mustard

¼ cup (60 mL) finely diced onion

½ tsp (2 mL) salt

¼ tsp (1 mL) pepper

1 cup (250 mL) canola oil

Tip

Blanch peas by placing them into a saucepan of boiling water. Have a bowl of ice water at the ready, and when the peas have cooked for 2 minutes, drain them and put them into the ice water to chill and stop the cooking process.

Beer-brined Pork Chops

Serves 6 to 8

This method is probably one of the best for cooking any type of "lean white meat" or poultry. The brine seals in the moisture in the meat and adds flavour to it. It is imperative that you use kosher or sea salt, but feel free to use different seasonings. At Christmas time, I use rosemary and cinnamon in place of the other spices.

3 to 4 lbs (1.5 to 2 kg) pork loin, pork chops or other cut of pork

2 Tbsp (30 mL) canola oil

Brine

8 cups (2 L) water

1 x 350 mL bottle dark beer (e.g., Maudite or Alley Kat Pale Ale)

¾ cup (175 mL) kosher or sea salt

½ cup (125 mL) maple syrup

1 tsp (5 mL) cloves

½ tsp (2 mL) nutmeg

½ tsp (2 mL) allspice

1 bay leaf

Place all brine ingredients in a medium saucepan and bring to a rolling boil. Turn down heat and simmer for 10 to 20 minutes to develop all of the flavours. Cool mixture to room temperature, then refrigerate until cold. Pour the brine over the meat, and marinate it in a non-reactive bowl or pail for 1 to 2 hours per pound (30 minutes to 1 hour per kg) of meat. Remove meat from brine and rinse well under cold water; pat dry.

Preheat the barbecue to medium-high. Lightly coat the meat with canola oil and grill until desired doneness. Check the internal temperature with an instant-read thermometer: to be done, the meat should be around 150° F (65° C).

Tip

Don't forget to rinse the pork well after marinating.

Tip

Any cooking method may be used for the brined pork, from grilling to roasting. I like to serve pork medium-rare, but others might want to stick to the 150° F (65° C) mark.

Microbrewers across Canada are producing fantastic products widely available to beer connoisseurs. Check out what's available locally and give it a try.

Teriyaki-glazed Ribs

Serves 4

Ribs are one of the hardest things to master on the barbecue. There are many different methods you can try. You can boil the ribs first and then finish them on the barbecue (as with the recipe below). You can cook them entirely on the barbecue, keeping the heat low and slow the entire time—no higher than 250° F (120° C), and make sure to keep the ribs moist (spray or mist them every 30 minutes with apple cider). Or you can bake them in the oven at 300° F (150° C) for 1 hour on each side, and then just finish them on the barbecue. Try all these ways and see which one works best for you!

4 lbs (1.8 kg) back ribs

Teriyaki Glaze

½ cup (125 mL) teriyaki sauce

½ cup (125 mL) liquid honey

⅓ cup (75 mL) Dijon mustard

¼ cup (60 mL) Worcestershire sauce

1 Tbsp (15 mL) hot pepper sauce

5 cloves garlic, minced

Fill Dutch oven with 8 cups (2 L) of water and bring to a boil. Add ribs. Turn heat down to a simmer and let simmer for 20 minutes. Remove and put into a shallow dish.

Combine teriyaki sauce, honey, mustard, Worcestershire sauce, hot pepper sauce and garlic in a small pot. Simmer, uncovered, for about 10 minutes until sauce is reduced to a glaze-like consistency. Preheat barbecue to medium. Brush ribs with sauce and place, meat-side down, on greased grill. Flip every 5 minutes, brushing with sauce, for a total of 20 minutes. Remove from barbecue and cut into 3-bone portions.

Mustard-rubbed Pork Tenderloin

Serves 4

Pork tenderloin is one of the most economical meat choices out there, and it tastes wonderful, with virtually no prep. The only thing to remember: do not overcook it, because it will dry out. Pork and mustard make a great combination of flavours. Use your favourite brand of Dijon mustard in this recipe—I like to use roasted garlic–flavoured grainy mustard as well. I also tuck rosemary sprigs in when I tie my roast, but you can simply stuff the sprigs into the barbecue or mix chopped herbs into the Mustard Rub.

2 pork tenderloins, approximately 1 lb (500 g) each

Mustard Rub
¼ cup (60 mL) Dijon mustard

1 Tbsp (15 mL) grainy mustard

1 Tbsp (15 mL) olive oil

salt and pepper

Mix rub ingredients together in a small bowl.

Slather the pork with the rub, making sure you thoroughly coat each pork tenderloin. Let them rest on a plate while the barbecue heats up.

Preheat the barbecue to high. Grill pork tenderloins for 7 minutes, rolling the meat around to ensure even cooking. Flip and cook for another 7 minutes, turning once. After that, turn the heat off, close the lid and let the meat rest for 5 minutes. Use an instant-read thermometer to make sure the meat's internal temperature is above 145° F (63° C). Carve into 4 equal pieces and serve.

Quebec and Ontario are the country's biggest pork producers. In the age of factory farms, it's somehow reassuring to know that 98 percent of pig farms in Canada are family owned and operated.

Pulled Pork

Serves 8 to 10

This recipe is not for the faint of heart. Although the method is easy, the cooking time is quite long, 8 to 12 hours, depending on the size of the roast. It's well worth the effort.

1 x 5 lb (2.3 kg) pork butt roast

hamburger buns

coleslaw (see Tip)

barbecue sauce

Seasoning Rub

¼ cup (60 mL) brown sugar

¼ cup (60 mL) seasoning salt

¼ cup (60 mL) paprika

1 Tbsp (15 mL) chili powder

2 tsp (10 mL) freshly ground pepper

1 tsp (5 mL) ground coriander

1 tsp (5 mL) ground cumin

1 tsp (5 mL) granulated onion

½ tsp (2 mL) cayenne pepper

In a bowl, mix all rub ingredients and then rub into the pork. Refrigerate for 1 hour.

Meanwhile, set up your barbecue for indirect heating: preheat one side to low—no higher than 250° F (120° C), and leave the other side off. Place the roast in the barbecue on the off side, and cook for 8 to 12 hours.

When the meat is done, it will pull apart with a fork.

To serve, stuff the meat into hamburger buns and top with coleslaw. Barbecue sauce, such as the Ancho Chili Barbecue Sauce (p. 118), is great with the pork.

Tip

Pouring the Ranch Dressing from the Potato Salad recipe (p. 48) over shredded cabbage makes great coleslaw.

Tip

A smoke box or foil pouch filled with aromatic hardwood chips will add a smoky flavour to the meat. Poke the foil pouch a few times to help release the fragrant aroma.

Grilled Sausages and Onions

Serves 6

Sausages are the essential guy food! One of the problems with them is their high fat content... Yeah! Gotta love them. They can be hard to grill, so I start mine in a cast iron pan with a layer of onions and beer, and then add more onions and the rest of the beer. Sausage lovers in Canada are particularly lucky, because all across the country are little corners of people who make some sort of traditional sausage, ranging from Greek, to German, to Italian, to Portuguese. In this recipe, use Italian sausage, chorizo, whatever you like.

2 lbs (1 kg) onions, thinly sliced

1 bottle dark beer

3 to 4 lbs (1.5 to 2 kg) raw sausages

1 tsp (5 mL) chopped fresh thyme

2 Tbsp (30 mL) honey

6 sub buns

your choice of condiments

Preheat one side of the barbecue to medium, the other side to hot. Line the bottom of a cast iron pan with a thin layer of sliced onions and pour in enough beer to just cover them.

Poke each sausage 3 or 4 times with a pin or small knife, and place in the pan with the beer and onions. Put the pan on the hot side of the barbecue and bring to a boil. Gently poach sausages for about 10 minutes or until they change colour and become firm. Remove from pan and place on medium side of the grill. Cook for about 15 minutes until done or until their internal temperature reaches 160° F (71° C).

Meanwhile, add the rest of the onions, the remaining beer and the thyme and honey to the cast iron pan. Cook over high heat until all of the liquid is evaporated and onions are done. If the sausages finish cooking before the onions, put them on top of everything in the cast iron pan as the onions continue to cook.

To serve, cut sausages in half lengthwise, put them in the buns and pile onions and your choice of condiments on top.

Vietnamese Pork the Canadian Way

Serves 2 to 4

Vietnamese food is one of the fastest growing food groups in Canada and, since there are still not a lot of Vietnamese restaurants around, everyone wants to know how the sweet, tangy sauce is made. Look for the ingredients in your neighbourhood supermarket or an Asian specialty food shop. This recipe brings the sweet spiciness of Vietnamese pork right into your own backyard. Pair this pork dish with a cold noodle salad, coleslaw or grilled peppers.

1 lb (500 g) thin-cut pork chops, or pork loin, cut ½ inch (1 cm) thick

Marinade

2 Tbsp (30 mL) diced onions

1 Tbsp (15 mL) diced lemongrass

¼ cup (60 mL) brown sugar

½ cup (125 mL) water

1 Tbsp (15 mL) fish sauce

1 Tbsp (15 mL) soy sauce

2 Tbsp (30 mL) canola oil

Pan-fry onions and lemongrass until soft. Add remaining marinade ingredients and bring to a gentle simmer for 5 minutes. When the mixture has cooled down, marinate pork in it for 1 hour.

Meanwhile, preheat the barbecue to medium-high. Grill pork chops for about 3 minutes. Rotate meat a quarter turn and cook for another 2 minutes to create grill marks. Flip the meat and cook for 3 minutes, then rotate and cook for another 2 minutes, or until desired doneness.

Drumsticks Two Ways

Serves 6 as appetizers, with sauce left over

Drumsticks are very versatile grill food. Try them with the Hot Sauce or the Thai Sauce; the cooking method is the same for both. You can also use wings, split and tips reserved and frozen for some future chicken broth event, but drumsticks are easier and better in this recipe.

2 lbs (1 kg) drumsticks

Hot Sauce

½ cup (125 mL) Barbecue Rub (p. 56)

½ tsp (2 mL) cayenne (more if you like)

⅔ cup (150 mL) hot sauce (use your favourite kind)

Thai Sauce

½ cup (125 mL) Ketjap Manis (Indonesian soy sauce)

1 Tbsp (15 mL) Sambal Oelek (Asian chili sauce)

¼ cup (60 mL) lime juice

1 Tbsp (15 mL) chopped garlic

1 Tbsp (15 mL) rice vinegar

1 Tbsp (15 mL) sugar

1 Tbsp (15 mL) fish sauce

For drumsticks with Hot Sauce, toss the drumsticks with the rub, cayenne and hot sauce in a large bowl. Marinate, refrigerated, for half an hour.

For drumsticks with Thai Sauce, whisk together all Thai sauce ingredients in a small bowl. Toss the drumsticks in a large bowl with ¼ cup (60 mL) Thai Sauce. Let marinate, refrigerated, for 1 hour. Reserve the rest of the sauce.

Preheat the barbecue to medium-high. Grill all drumsticks for about 20 to 30 minutes until brown and crispy. When the drumsticks with the Thai Sauce are done, toss them in 2 batches in a large bowl with the remaining sauce, making sure they are saucy.

Sit back and enjoy, using the buttermilk Ranch Dressing (p. 48) as a dip.

Tip

Ketjap Manis, Sambal Oelek and fish sauce are available in your grocery store or Asian markets.

Drumettes are way better than wings—they're way more economical. This recipe is perfect when you have guests arriving in groups. Just grill a batch at a time and hand them out as people arrive.

Greek Chicken Breast with Feta and Pepper Relish

Serves 4

Lemon, garlic, honey and oregano are truly classic flavours in Greek cooking. In this recipe, you can use any fresh herb you like, or try a combination of your favourite herbs for a fantastic flavour. The red wine vinegar gives a tang to the chicken and helps to seal in the moisture.

4 skinless, boneless chicken breasts, pounded slightly to same thickness

Marinade

½ cup (125 mL) olive oil

2 Tbsp (30 mL) crushed garlic

1 Tbsp (15 mL) chopped fresh oregano

2 tsp (10 mL) red wine vinegar

1 Tbsp (15 mL) honey

¼ tsp (1 mL) salt

¼ tsp (1 mL) pepper

juice from ½ lemon

Put chicken into a sealable plastic bag. Mix all marinade ingredients in a bowl and pour over the chicken. Marinate in the fridge for at least 2 hours but no longer than 6.

Preheat the barbecue to medium-high. Remove chicken from marinade and grill for 5 to 7 minutes per side, flipping once.

To make the relish, julienne peppers and set aside with the onions. In a large bowl, mix together the vinegar, oil, garlic and oregano. Toss the feta into the dressing, maintaining some chunks, then toss with the peppers and onions. Season to taste with salt and pepper.

Serve chicken on plates or a platter topped with Feta and Pepper Relish.

Feta and Pepper Relish

3 bell peppers (mixed colours), quartered, seeded and stem removed

¼ cup (60 mL) sliced red onion

1 Tbsp (15 mL) balsamic vinegar

¼ cup (60 mL) olive oil

1 tsp (5 mL) crushed garlic

2 Tbsp (30 mL) chopped fresh oregano

½ cup (125 mL) crumbled feta

salt and pepper

Coconut Pesto-stuffed Chicken Breasts

Serves 4

A cooked-to-perfection dish from the Company's Coming collection. Whisk friends to the tropics with chicken breasts stuffed with a coconut pesto. The coconut rum wash gives the chicken a deep caramelized colour and just a touch of "spirited" flavour.

4 boneless, skinless chicken breast halves

Coconut Pesto

1½ cups (375 mL) fresh basil, lightly packed

⅓ cup (75 mL) chopped macadamia nuts

⅓ cup (75 mL) medium sweetened coconut

¼ cup (60 mL) pineapple juice

2 Tbsp (30 mL) lime juice

salt

Rub

1 tsp (5 mL) canola oil

½ tsp (2 mL) paprika

½ tsp (2 mL) seasoned salt

¼ tsp (1 mL) pepper

¼ cup (60 mL) coconut rum

1½ Tbsp (25 mL) brown sugar, packed

Preheat barbecue to medium. In a blender or food processor, process Coconut Pesto ingredients until a thick paste forms.

Cut slits horizontally in chicken breasts to form pockets and fill with basil mixture. Secure with wooden picks.

Combine rub ingredients and rub over chicken.

Combine rum and brown sugar. Grill chicken for 5 to 6 minutes per side, brushing occasionally with rum mixture, until chicken is no longer pink inside. Cover with foil and let stand for 5 minutes.

Tip

Garnish with mixed baby greens and grilled pineapple.

Grilled Chicken with Grapefruit Drizzle

Serves 4

Barbecued chicken is one the best summer treats, but sometimes the sauce can be a little too heavy for a hot summer day. Everyone has heard about lemon chicken, but try my chicken with grapefruit and see what you think. Crisp chicken bathed with the sweet tanginess of grapefruit is a perfect hot summer barbecue.

1 broiler chicken, cut in half, backbone removed

1 Tbsp (15 mL) canola oil

2 Tbsp (30 mL) seasoning salt or Barbecue Rub (p. 56)

Grapefruit Drizzle Sauce

1 grapefruit

½ cup (125 mL) extra-virgin olive oil

1 Tbsp (15 mL) sherry vinegar

¼ cup (60 mL) chopped parsley

Preheat the barbecue to medium. Rub chicken with canola oil, then season with seasoning salt or rub, making sure you coat well. Grill chicken for about 15 minutes per side, or until golden brown and crispy.

While the chicken is cooking, remove the peel from the grapefruit and cut the grapefruit into segments. Set aside. In a bowl, mix together the olive oil, vinegar, parsley and whatever juice you can squeeze out of the grapefruit peel, blending well.

Place the grilled chicken on a platter, pour the sauce over top and serve with the grapefruit segments.

Tip

To crisp up the chicken skin, turn the heat on the barbecue up to high for the last 5 to 10 minutes of cooking, but be wary of flare-ups—you don't want to set your eyebrows on fire.

Grapefruit is a particularly healthy treat among those wishing to reduce the fat and cholesterol in their diets.

Tandoori Chicken Thigh Skewers

Serves 6 to 8

Tandoori chicken is truly a culinary gift from our Indian friends. It is traditionally cooked whole on a stick in a Tandoori oven, which can reach 5000° F (2760° C)! Replicating that heat is a bit of a challenge with the domestic barbecues most of us cook with in this country, but this recipe works well with boneless chicken thighs. I think they have better flavour and certainly stay moister in this application.

3 lbs (1.5 kg) boneless chicken thighs

12 bamboo skewers

Marinade

2 Tbsp (30 mL) crushed garlic

3 Tbsp (45 mL) crushed ginger

3 Tbsp (45 mL) canola oil

1 Tbsp (15 mL) vinegar

1 Tbsp (15 mL) red chili powder or paprika

2 tsp (10 mL) cardamom seeds

2 tsp (10 mL) ground bay leaves

2 tsp (10 mL) ground cinnamon

2 tsp (10 mL) ground cloves

2 tsp (10 mL) ground ginger

1 cup (250 mL) plain yogurt

Mix ingredients for the marinade together in a large bowl. Add chicken and marinate in the fridge for 1 to 3 hours. Meanwhile, soak bamboo skewers in water so they don't catch fire on the grill.

Preheat the barbecue to medium-high. Skewer the thighs, leaving a little space between each piece to allow the chicken to cook. Grill for 5 to 7 minutes per side. Turn off the heat and close the lid. Check the skewers after 5 minutes to make sure that the chicken is fully cooked. Serve with Naan bread and rice.

Tip

To check the chicken thighs for doneness, just cut into the thickest piece. The juices should run clear if the meat is done. Or use an instant-read thermometer.

Turkey "Pastrami"

Serves 6 to 8

Why do most Canadians only have turkey at celebrations? Turkey can be eaten any time of the year—in this recipe, a turkey breast is brined and then slow-roasted with a rub reminiscent of the deli classic. Turkey pastrami is fantastic in a sandwich. Slice it thinly, pile it on bread and top it with sauerkraut, and there you go. You can also serve it with your family's favourite trimmings.

1 x 2 to 3 lbs (1 to 1.5 kg) turkey breast, skin on

Brine

8 cups (2 L) water

½ cup (125 mL) kosher salt

1 Tbsp (15 mL) Szechwan peppercorns

¼ cup (60 mL) brown sugar

2 Tbsp (30 mL) balsamic vinegar

"Pastrami" Rub

¼ cup (60 mL) paprika

3 Tbsp (45 mL) coriander seeds

3 Tbsp (45 mL) brown sugar

3 Tbsp (45 mL) black peppercorns

2 Tbsp (30 mL) Szechwan peppercorns

Place water, salt, peppercorns, brown sugar and vinegar in a medium pot and bring to a simmer. Cool to room temperature, then chill until ice cold. Add the turkey breast, cover and refrigerate for 6 hours.

Remove from fridge and rinse well.

Coarsely grind rub ingredients in a coffee grinder, mortar and pestle or blender (or use the back of a frying pan). Rub 2 to 3 Tbsp (30 to 45 mL) over the entire turkey breast.

Preheat one side of the barbecue to medium-low. Place the turkey breast on the side with no heat, close the lid and maintain the temperature at 300° F (150° C). Check with an instant-read thermometer after 2 hours. You want the turkey to reach an internal temperature of 160° F (71° C). When it is done, remove from heat and let rest for 15 minutes before carving.

Hot or cold, turkey pastrami slices are wonderful in sandwiches.

Nick's Teriyaki Steak

Serves 6 to 8

Dad didn't do a whole lot of cooking at home but he did barbecue a lot, and he did a fine job of it. I think this recipe, one of his favourites, came from a relative of ours in the Toronto area. It looks simple, and it is. As a professional chef, I have tried to "improve" on it, but some things just work and this recipe is one of those things. The secret is to buy really thick steak—and marinate it overnight.

1 x 2-inch (5 cm) thick sirloin steak, about 3 lbs (1.5 kg)

Marinade

1 cup (250 mL) soy sauce (Chinese, not Japanese)

½ cup (125 mL) freshly squeezed lemon juice

3 Tbsp (45 mL) liquid honey

2 tsp (10 mL) garlic powder

Mix marinade ingredients together in a small bowl. Place steak in a plastic sealable bag and pour in marinade. Refrigerate overnight, flipping once.

Preheat the barbecue to medium-high. Blot steak dry and grill for about 15 minutes per side, flipping once. The steak is incredibly thick, so it will probably take about 30 minutes to reach medium-rare. Once steak is cooked, allow it to relax for 10 minutes—it will not get cold. Carve into ½-inch (1 cm) slices. I like to serve it with Grilled Sourdough Bread (p. 20) and Caesar salad.

Strip Loin with Blue Cheese

Serves 4

The New York strip loin is one of the best steak cuts around. It is so named because when properly cut, it looks like Manhattan Island. There are two keys to preparing this steak: allow the meat to come to room temperature before you cook it, and coat it well with the barbecue rub.

2 x 12 oz (340 g) New York steaks, room temperature

½ cup (125 mL) Barbecue Rub (p. 56)

4 oz (115 g) blue cheese

Preheat the barbecue to high. Place rub in a large plastic bag, and coat steaks, one at a time, with the rub. Make sure they are coated well.

Grill steaks for approximately 7 minutes per side, flipping once. The rub might cause flare-ups, so watch carefully.

When steaks are cooked, remove from heat and crumble half the blue cheese over top of each steak. Let the meat sit for a few minutes while the cheese warms. Carve steaks into 1-inch (2.5 cm) slices, and serve with sliced tomatoes and baked potatoes if you wish.

 You have to look into the growing number of pasture-raised and organic premium beef growers in the country. For example, the Blue Goose Cattle Company in the Cariboo area of British Columbia is raising beef that is finding its way into fine restaurants and high-end butcher shops around the province.

Chateaubriand with Horseradish Crème Frâiche

Serves 4

Beef tenderloin straight off the barbecue—could there be a better treat? Especially if you can get beef that is Black Angus... The butt end of the tenderloin is the chateaubriand, and brought to the table and carved there, it makes a great presentation. When cooked, this piece of meat will be a nice bright pink in the middle. Make the Horseradish Crème Frâiche while the meat is cooking, so it will be ready to dollop on for the presentation.

1 x 2 lb (1 kg) beef tenderloin, butt end

1 Tbsp (15 mL) canola oil

1 Tbsp (15 mL) salt

1 tsp (5 mL) cracked black pepper

Horseradish Crème Frâiche

1 cup (250 mL) crème frâiche or sour cream

1 Tbsp (15 mL) creamed horseradish

1 Tbsp (15 mL) lemon juice

½ tsp (2 mL) cracked black pepper

Rub meat with canola oil. Season with salt and pepper, and let sit at room temperature for about 1 hour.

Preheat one side of the barbecue to hot and the other side to low. Quickly sear meat on the hot side of the barbecue for about 5 minutes per side. Move the meat to the low heat side and turn off the high heat side. Cook for another 20 minutes, flipping once, until the meat reaches desired doneness.

Mix Horseradish Crème Frâiche ingredients together in a small bowl. Set aside.

Remove the meat to a cutting board and let sit for 15 minutes. Carve into 1-inch (2.5 cm) slices, and serve with a dollop of Horseradish Crème Frâiche on top.

〰 *Purists in Canada can grow horseradish but it kind of takes over the garden. The highly aromatic root can bring tears to a grown man's eyes. Save yourself the grief and use bottled horseradish.*

Veal Chops with Red Pepper Basil Butter

Serves 4 to 6

Milk-fed veal from Quebec is truly a culinary delight, but check local sources for supplies. The sweetness of red pepper and the intense freshness of basil is a perfect complement to the tender and sweet veal. For a red pepper spread, I like to use the brand Gloria, found in the Italian section of your supermarket. The secret to this dish is large, thick veal chops; they should each weigh in at upwards of 1 lb (500 g), so you can also carve the chop.

4 veal chops, frenched (see Tip)

1 Tbsp (15 mL) canola oil

salt and pepper

Red Pepper Basil Butter

1 cup (250 mL) butter, room temperature

2 Tbsp (30 mL) red pepper spread

1 Tbsp (15 mL) freshly squeezed lemon juice

2 Tbsp (30 mL) chopped fresh basil

In a small bowl, cream butter with the red pepper spread. Add lemon juice and mix together. Fold in chopped basil, and adjust seasoning if necessary. Set aside.

Preheat the barbecue to medium-high. Rub each veal chop with a little canola oil and season with salt and pepper. Grill for about 10 minutes per side, flipping once. Let the chops sit for 5 minutes. Place a big dollop of Red Pepper Basil Butter on top of each chop, let it melt, then serve.

Tip

Frenching is a technique used for decorative purposes on cuts of meat that have a bone exposed, like these veal chops. You use a knife to scrape away at the meat around the bone, making sure that it is clean and white. Alternatively, ask the butcher to french the chops for you.

Tequila-marinated Flat Iron Steak

Serves 4

This extremely tasty piece of meat lends itself well to marinating. Lime adds a burst of tang, tequila adds a subtle flavour, and the hint of spices make for a great-tasting steak. Do not overcook the meat, and remember to slice against the grain. Flat iron steak is a cut from the blade, so named because it's shaped like a flat iron. If you can't find a flat iron steak, just use flank steak.

2 lbs (1 kg) flat iron or flank steak

Marinade

1 Tbsp (15 mL) chopped garlic

1 tsp (5 mL) crushed red chili flakes

about ¼ cup (60 mL) lime juice plus zest from 1 lime

2 Tbsp (30 mL) tequila

¼ cup (60 mL) extra-virgin olive oil

Mix marinade ingredients together in a small bowl. Reserve 2 Tbsp (30 mL) of the marinade and place the rest with the steak in a sealable plastic bag. Refrigerate for 4 to 6 hours.

Preheat the barbecue to high. Grill steak for about 3 to 4 minutes per side for medium-rare. Once flipped, brush steak with reserved marinade.

When finished cooking, let meat relax on a platter for 5 minutes, then slice across the grain and serve at once.

Tequila, with or without the worm, is one of those ingredients that have migrated north from Mexico to Canada. It goes really well in this marinade with chili flakes and lime. In fact, margaritas also go well with the steak.

Chipotle-braised Short Ribs

Serves 6, or 10 as an appetizer

Short ribs are meaty, beefy ribs. They need a long, slow cooking time, and they're not typically cooked on the grill. I dust my ribs with a dry rub and then slow-cook them over indirect heat for 3 to 4 hours, or until the meat falls off the bone. Because these short ribs are so rich, you don't need many to make a great meal.

3 lbs (1.5 kg) short ribs, trimmed of almost all fat

Chipotle Rub

3 Tbsp (45 mL) dried oregano

2 tsp (10 mL) dried parsley flakes

2 Tbsp (30 mL) dried thyme leaves

2 Tbsp (30 mL) kosher salt

1 Tbsp (15 mL) cracked black pepper

2 tsp (10 mL) ground chipotle powder

1 tsp (5 mL) garlic powder

1 Tbsp (15 mL) brown sugar

Preheat one side of barbecue to low and leave the other side off. Mix rub ingredients together in a small bowl and place in a plastic bag. In small batches, dredge the short ribs in the rub, and place on the off side of barbecue. When all ribs are on the grill, close the lid and let cook for 3 hours, checking about every 45 minutes and flipping the meat.

During the cooking time, you may want to "mop" the ribs with equal amounts of beer and your favourite barbecue sauce. When the ribs are done—when the meat falls off the bones—slather on some more of the beer and barbecue sauce mixture, serve and enjoy.

Sirloin with Warm Mushroom Salad

Serves 4

Sirloin is such a quintessentially Canadian meat to barbecue, and the mushrooms go so well with it. This salad is made of mushrooms that are grilled, then dressed and served at room temperature on top of the steak. The whole garlic infuses the mushrooms but doesn't overwhelm the dish. The salad can be served with any grilled meat.

4 sirloin steaks, 1 inch (2.5 cm) thick

1 Tbsp (15 mL) canola oil

salt and pepper

Mushroom Salad

1 lb (500 g) shiitake mushrooms, stems removed

1 x ½ lb (250 g) small portobello mushroom, sliced ½-inch (1 cm) thick

¼ cup (60 mL) extra-virgin olive oil

2 cloves garlic

¼ cup (60 mL) diced red onion

3 Tbsp (45 mL) mushroom soy sauce

cracked black pepper

Preheat the barbecue to medium-high. In a large bowl, toss mushrooms with olive oil to coat well, and grill them for 2 to 3 minutes per side or until done. Return the grilled mushrooms to the bowl and toss with the garlic, onions, mushroom soy sauce and pepper. Let stand at room temperature 1 hour, which gives you plenty of time to grill the steaks.

Rub steak with canola oil and season with salt and pepper. Grill steaks for 3 to 4 minutes per side, flipping once. Let relax for 5 minutes, then top with Mushroom Salad and serve.

Tip

Leave the cloves of garlic whole so they can be removed before serving.

If you want to serve this recipe as an appetizer, just slice up the meat and serve it on a platter.

Tuscan-style Grilled Top Blade

Serves 4

Canadians eat enough Italian food to know that Italians like to cook food in very straightforward and simple ways—with flavour and taste being the key elements. The meat used in this recipe is not one of the most tender cuts available. It comes from the shoulder of the animal and is meaty and rich, but it does have a little chew. However, the preparation is simple, and extra garlic can be added if you like.

3 lbs (1.5 kg) blade steaks

juice from 1 lemon

2 Tbsp (30 mL) extra-virgin olive oil

Marinade

3 sprigs fresh rosemary

3 sprigs fresh sage

3 sprigs fresh thyme

½ cup (125 mL) olive oil

1 Tbsp (15 mL) crushed garlic

1 Tbsp (15 mL) red wine vinegar

salt and pepper

Rough chop herbs, and in a small bowl mix them with olive oil, garlic and vinegar. Season with salt and pepper. Place steaks in a non-reactive glass dish or sealable plastic bag, and pour marinade over top. Refrigerate for 6 hours, flipping steaks once.

Preheat the barbecue to high and grill steaks for 3 to 4 minutes per side for medium-rare. When the steaks are cooked, let them relax on a platter for a few minutes. Carve into ½-inch (1 cm) slices, and drizzle with freshly squeezed lemon juice and olive oil.

Tip

Fresh and hearty herbs are important to the outcome of this recipe. If you like, place sprigs of herbs right on the grill, and lay the steaks on top so that the herbs will help flavour the meat as it cooks. Make sure the herbs are slightly moistened before you put them on the grill.

Chimichurri Burgers

Serves 6

Who doesn't like a burger? Burger parties are a fun idea when entertaining in the summer, so instead of worrying about cooking a steak to the proper doneness, do burgers. I like to keep my burger very simple: no binders, and no eggs. The burgers should all be cooked to the same degree of doneness, and people can choose their own combinations of condiments. The Chimichurri sauce brings a taste of Argentina to our barbecues, and Argentinians are well-known for their beef barbecues.

Burgers

2 lbs (1 kg) ground beef
(extra lean is too lean)

⅓ cup (75 mL) Chimichurri
Sauce (p. 122); reserve
2 Tbsp (30 mL)

1 tsp (5 mL) salt

cracked black pepper

slices of cheese, your
favourite kind (optional)

½ cup (125 mL)
mayonnaise

6 hamburger buns, or
12 slices of good bread

2 large tomatoes, cut into
½-inch (1 cm) slices

1 white onion, cut into
¼-inch (0.5 cm) slices

fresh lettuce

Mix meat, Chimichurri sauce, salt and pepper together in a large bowl until well combined. Shape into 6 patties and refrigerate for 1 hour.

Preheat the barbecue to medium-high. Grill burgers for 5 to 7 minutes per side, or until an internal temperature of 160° F (71° C) is reached. Put slices of cheese on the burgers, if desired. Turn off the heat and close the lid.

To assemble, mix reserved Chimichurri sauce and mayonnaise together in a small bowl. Spread some sauce on the bottom of each bun or slice of bread. Put the burgers on and serve with tomatoes, onions, lettuce and desired condiments.

Tip

Burgers hold together better on the grill if they've been refrigerated for about 1 hour beforehand.

If you don't like beef burgers, simply use turkey or pork. Chimichurri sauce will keep any type of burger meat moist.

Blue Cheese Beer Burgers

Serves 8

It's impossible to talk about barbecuing without throwing in a couple good burger recipes. Perfect for a pre-game party or a post-game get-together, these hearty burgers hold a hint of the beer you can serve with the meal. The Stilton adds a pleasing, creamy sharpness to the burgers, which are a favourite of the Company's Coming Test Kitchen.

2 lbs (1 kg) lean ground beef

1 cup (250 mL) finely chopped onion

½ cup (125 mL) fine dry bread crumbs

⅓ cup (75 mL) stout beer

1 tsp (5 mL) celery salt

1 tsp (5 mL) garlic powder

½ tsp (2 mL) pepper

6 oz (170 g) Stilton cheese, sliced

8 onion buns, split

Combine first 7 ingredients and divide into 8 portions. Shape portions into patties, about 4 inches (10 cm) in diameter. Chill, covered, for 1 hour. Grill patties on direct medium heat for about 5 minutes per side until internal temperature reaches 160° F (71° C). Top with cheese during final minute of cooking.

Serve patties in buns.

Tip

Patties can be made up to six hours in advance.

Tip

Try something different and garnish your burgers with pickled beet slices and tomato slices. You can also experiment and use Harvard or roasted beets instead of pickled ones.

Grilled Lobster

Serves 8

Nothing says summer like our own Atlantic lobster. I like a steamed or boiled lobster like everyone else, but you have to try it barbecued: lobster takes on a whole different flavour when you put it on the grill. To grill lobster, you can crack the claws, remove the meat and place it in the shells, or you can simply parboil the claws whole and finish them on the grill. The latter provides for a better presentation.

4 x 1½ lb (750 g) live lobsters

1 cup (250 mL) butter

2 Tbsp (30 mL) chopped chives

salt and pepper

1 lemon, quartered

Preheat the barbecue to medium-high. In a small saucepan on the side burner or grill, melt butter and add chives. Set aside.

Split each lobster (see Tip); remove intestines, stomach and gills from the body cavity, thus leaving an empty shell. Remove the claws where they attach to the body. Crush the claws (whack them heartily with a heavy knife), remove the meat and place it in the shells.

Place each lobster, cut-side up, on the grill. Cook for 15 to 20 minutes, basting with chive butter frequently, until meat is opaque.

Place lobsters on a large platter and season with salt and pepper. Serve with remaining chive butter and lemon quarters.

Tip

If you're squeamish about splitting live lobsters, have your fishmonger perform the task for you.

"Vegetarian-style" Surf and Turf

Serves 4

Sweet shrimp, tender scallops, mussels, and the ever-popular East Coast treat, lobster, nestled on a grilled "beefy" portobello mushroom, dripping with chive lemon butter—what could be a better substitute for the more traditional beef?

1 cup (250 mL) butter

2 Tbsp (30 mL) chopped chives

2 Tbsp (30 mL) freshly squeezed lemon juice

4 portabella mushrooms

2 Tbsp (30 mL) canola oil

salt and pepper

2 lobster tails, split

½ lb (250 g) large scallops

½ lb (250 g) large shrimp

1 lb (500 g) mussels, de-bearded (see Tip, p. 26)

cracked pepper

Preheat the barbecue to medium-high. In a small saucepan on the side burner, melt the butter with the chives and lemon juice, and mix well. Set aside.

Brush the portobellos with 1 Tbsp (15 mL) canola oil and season with salt and pepper. In a large bowl, toss lobster tails with some of the remaining oil; repeat with scallops, then shrimp and then mussels.

Grill portobellos for 3 to 5 minutes per side, or until done, and keep warm. Grill lobster cut-side up, basting with the chive butter for about 10 minutes, until flesh turns opaque and firm. Grill scallops for 2 minutes per side, or until they turn opaque. Keep warm.

Grill shrimp for 2 minutes per side, or until they turn pink. Cook mussels by simply throwing them on the grill until they open.

To assemble, lay out 4 plates. Place a mushroom cap on each plate, and top it with half a lobster tail and the rest of the seafood, divided among the plates. To serve, crack some fresh pepper on top and drizzle with remaining chive butter.

Hobo Halibut with Honey Vinaigrette

Serves 4

Camping is a great summer pastime for a lot of Canadians, and this meal is a simple and convenient one-package dinner. Just wrap all ingredients in foil and place them on your campfire (or on your barbecue at home). Once the fish is done, everyone can eat right out of the foil packages, thus saving someone from having to wash dishes. Be sure the fire is not too hot, or the fish will burn.

4 square sheets of foil

oil for brushing foil

1 lb (500 g) baby potatoes, quartered

1 lb (500 g) asparagus, trimmed

1 onion, sliced

½ lb (250 g) cherry tomatoes

4 halibut fillets

fresh herbs, any kind

salt and pepper

Honey Vinaigrette

1 cup (250 mL) olive oil

⅓ cup (75 mL) vinegar

juice from 1 lemon

1 Tbsp (15 mL) honey

2 cloves garlic, peeled but whole

1 tsp (5 mL) dried thyme

1 tsp (5 mL) dried oregano

salt and pepper

Blend all Honey Vinaigrette ingredients together in a jar and set aside (see Tip).

Have your campfire or barbecue at medium-high to hot. Brush sheets of foil with oil to prevent food from sticking. Divide the vegetables among the sheets. Make sure the ingredients are in the middle of each sheet. Place the halibut fillets on top of the vegetables and drizzle each pile with your choice of fresh herbs and ¼ cup (60 mL) Honey Vinaigrette. Season to taste with salt and pepper. Join corners of each foil square to seal tightly and place packages on grill. Cook for 15 minutes, until fish flakes, and serve.

Tip

Leftover vinaigrette can be stored in the fridge for up to 6 weeks and used as needed.

Seared Tuna Steak with Sesame Ginger Sauce

Serves 4

Sesame, ginger and sake provide a Japanese essence to fresh tuna steak in this innovative recipe from the Company's Coming library. The charred smokiness of the baby bok choy takes the overall taste to another level.

4 x 4 oz (115 g) tuna steaks, about 1 inch (2.5 cm) thick

8 whole baby bok choy, halved lengthwise

Sesame Ginger Sauce

2 Tbsp (30 mL) ponzu sauce (see Tip)

2 Tbsp (30 mL) tahini

1 Tbsp (15 mL) finely grated ginger root

1 Tbsp (15 mL) sake

1 Tbsp (15 mL) sesame oil

1 clove garlic, minced

½ tsp (2 mL) dry mustard

Marinade

¼ cup (60 mL) ponzu sauce

2 Tbsp (30 mL) sake

2 Tbsp (30 mL) sesame oil

1 Tbsp (15 mL) finely chopped fresh cives

Combine Sesame Ginger Sauce ingredients. Set aside (see Tip).

Combine marinade ingredients. Reserve ¼ cup (60 mL). Pour remaining mixture into a large sealable freezer bag. Add tuna and chill for 30 minutes. Drain and discard marinade.

Preheat the barbecue to medium-high. Grill tuna and bok choy for about 3 minutes per side, brushing with reserved marinade, until tuna is medium-rare and bok choy is tender-crisp. Serve with Sesame Ginger Sauce.

Tip

Prepare the sauce in advance and store in the refrigerator. Bring to room temperature before serving.

Find ponzu sauce in the Asian section of most grocery stores. Ponzu sauce is a mixture of soy sauce, lemon juice or rice vinegar, kombu (seaweed), dried bonito flakes and mirin or sake. A common ingredient in Japanese cooking, ponzu is generally used as a dipping sauce.

Bison Rib-eye with Mango Chutney Peppercorn Sauce

Serves 4

More than a century after the plains bison was decimated in western Canada, farmed bison is making a heroic comeback on the menus of the nation. Bison is wonderful meat; if you can obtain your bison from growers in Manitoba, so much the better. Bison is lower in cholesterol than beef, and it has a somewhat sweeter taste. The Mango Chutney Peppercorn Sauce is also slightly sweet and complements the bison well, and the peppercorns give the sauce a hint of fire. Remember not to overcook the bison (no more than medium) because the meat is low in fat.

4 x 10 oz (280 g) bison rib-eye steaks

1 Tbsp (15 mL) canola oil

salt and pepper

Mango Chutney Peppercorn Sauce

1 cup (250 mL) beef stock

½ cup (125 mL) mango chutney (bottled Earl Grey chutney is my favourite brand)

1 Tbsp (15 mL) green peppercorns

¼ cup (60 mL) red wine

salt and pepper (optional)

Place all sauce ingredients in a saucepan on the grill or side burner. Cook for 15 minutes, or until slightly reduced, and season with salt and pepper, if needed. Set aside.

Preheat the barbecue to medium-high. Rub the bison steaks with canola oil and season with salt and pepper. Grill for 5 minutes per side, flipping once. Let rest for 5 minutes. Place each steak on a plate and nap Mango Chutney Peppercorn Sauce over top. Serve immediately.

If you don't want to use red wine in this recipe, just use a beer from your favourite local micro-brewery. They're all over the country nowadays.

Coffee-marinated Duck Breast

Serves 4

Tender and plump, Muscovy duck breast is delicious—you don't have to load that shotgun come fall to get a great quality duck anymore. Because duck contains a lot of fat, I tend to make this recipe in a cast iron pan to render all the fat out and to get the skin nice and crispy. The coffee in this recipe not only adds flavour, but the caffeine also acts as a natural tenderizer.

4 duck breasts, trimmed of fat

3 cups (750 mL) espresso or strong coffee, ice cold; ¼ cup (60 mL) reserved for sauce

½ cup (125 mL) Ancho Chili Barbecue Sauce (p. 118)

1 tsp (5 mL) honey

Score the duck breast by lightly cutting into the skin in a criss-cross pattern, about 4 times each way; be careful not to cut all the way through the skin. Place duck and coffee in a sealable plastic bag and refrigerate for 6 hours, flipping once.

Preheat a cast iron pan to medium-high over grill or side burner. Remove duck from the coffee and pat dry. Place skin-side down in the pan and cook for 10 minutes, or until the skin is dark golden brown. Remove any excess fat from the pan. Flip duck over and cook for another 7 to 10 minutes for medium. Remove duck and keep warm.

Remove all fat from the pan. Add reserved coffee, barbecue sauce and honey to pan and heat until combined. Cut the breasts in half lengthwise and ladle sauce over each half. Serve immediately.

Elk Tenderloin with Wild Blueberry Sauce

Serves 4

Elk—fast becoming a new favourite across Canada—is being raised domestically and can be found in specialty butcher stores almost anywhere in the country. Elk has a great texture; it's more earthy than beefy in taste. Because the meat is so lean, I have combined it with a blueberry sauce that has some sweetness.

4 elk tenderloin fillets, about 8 oz (250 g) each

1 Tbsp (15 mL) canola oil

salt and pepper

4 pieces prosciutto or bacon

Wild Blueberry Sauce

1 Tbsp (15 mL) butter

2 Tbsp (30 mL) finely chopped onion

½ cup (125 mL) Port or red wine

2 Tbsp (30 mL) red wine vinegar

1 Tbsp (15 mL) red currant jelly

1 cup (250 mL) wild blueberries, saskatoons, or a mix

For the sauce, melt butter in a small saucepan and add onion. Cook until softened, about 5 minutes. Add the Port, vinegar and jelly, and cook for 10 minutes over medium heat, or until slightly reduced. Keep warm. Just before serving, add the berries.

Rub the tenderloins with canola oil and season with salt and pepper. Wrap each fillet with a piece of prosciutto (or bacon) and secure with a toothpick.

Preheat the barbecue to medium-high. Grill elk for 5 to 8 minutes per side, flipping once, for medium doneness. If you want to cook the meat longer, turn the grill off, close the lid and leave it for another 5 minutes. Elk dries out if it is cooked beyond medium. To serve, remove the toothpicks, put the fillets on a plate and ladle Wild Blueberry Sauce over top.

 Blueberries are one of the healthiest foods on the planet. You can find them fresh or frozen in just about any grocery store. Saskatoons make a great substitute, but you might need a bucket and the permission of a friendly farmer to harvest some wild berries.

Moroccan Lamb Chops

Serves 4

Lamb chops make a terrific appetizer or entrée. Try to buy your lamb locally: it's true that Salt Spring Island lamb is about the sweetest you can get, but growers in your area are bound to have a great quality product. For this dish, you can leave the lamb chops together as a rack or cook them individually. The nice thing about this type of meat is that it cooks very quickly and it comes with a bone—its own built-in "handle." The spices in this dish lend an exotic hint of Morocco to the meat.

20 lamb rib chops

1 Tbsp (15 mL) olive oil

Moroccan Rub

3 Tbsp (45 mL) cumin seeds

3 Tbsp (45 mL) cardamom

3 Tbsp (45 mL) coriander

1 Tbsp (15 mL) peppercorns

3 Tbsp (45 mL) kosher salt

1 Tbsp (15 mL) dried oregano

1 tsp (5 mL) dried thyme

1 tsp (5 mL) crushed red chili flakes

Preheat the barbecue to medium-high. Place cumin, cardamom, coriander and peppercorns in a coffee grinder or mortar and pestle (or use the bottom of a cast iron pan). Pulse or grind until a coarse grind is achieved. Put into a small bowl with kosher salt, oregano, thyme and chili flakes. Stir to combine well.

Rub the chops with olive oil and then the ground spices. Grill for 5 to 7 minutes per side, rotating once for grill marks.

Pistachio-dusted Leg of Lamb

Serves 6 to 8

Leg of lamb is a great thing to grill. It has lots of tender meat that absorbs marinades well. In addition, owing to the contour of the boneless leg, some parts of the meat will turn out more cooked than others, which will please everyone.

1 x 3 to 5 lb (1.5 to 2.3 kg) boneless leg of lamb

1 Tbsp (15 mL) grainy mustard (Brassica is my favourite)

2 Tbsp (30 mL) olive oil

2 Tbsp (30 mL) rough chopped fresh rosemary

¼ cup (60 mL) chopped garlic

2 Tbsp (30 mL) freshly squeezed lemon juice

1 cup (250 mL) yogurt

salt and pepper

1 cup (250 mL) finely crushed pistachio nuts

In a small bowl mix together mustard, oil, rosemary, garlic, lemon juice and yogurt. Smear mixture over lamb, pressing into all of the crevices. Refrigerate for 6 hours or overnight.

Preheat one side of the barbecue to medium-high and the other to low. Remove lamb from marinade and wipe off excess. Place meat on the medium-high side of the barbecue for 35 to 45 minutes for medium-rare. If flare-ups occur, move the meat to the low-heat side of the barbecue. If you like lamb cooked well done, turn the heat off, close the lid and let the meat cook for another 10 to 15 minutes.

Take meat off grill and let sit for 15 minutes. Dust with pistachios and carve into ½-inch (1 cm) slices.

Tip

This recipe is awesome when drizzled with Pomegranate Vinaigrette (p. 128).

The pistachio coating can be used on pork or chicken with very tasty results.

Lamb Burgers with Basil Mayonnaise

Serves 6

We always think of ground lamb being in lasagna and casseroles. This recipe is a great way to enjoy Canadian-grown lamb, from the West Coast or the East Coast or in between. These burgers are so tasty they'll surely become a new family tradition.

2 lbs (1 kg) ground lamb

1 Tbsp (15 mL) salt

½ tsp (2 mL) pepper

6 burger buns

1 wheel Camembert, sliced vertically

6 tomatoes, thickly sliced

2 cups (500 mL) fried onions

Basil Mayonnaise

1 cup (250 mL) mayonnaise

¼ cup (60 mL) basil pesto

For Basil Mayonnaise, mix mayonnaise and pesto in a small bowl until well combined, then refrigerate until needed.

Mix lamb and salt and pepper together in a large bowl. Shape into balls, and flatten to form patties. Refrigerate until ready to grill.

Preheat the barbecue to medium-high. Grill burgers for about 7 minutes per side, flipping once. Remove to a platter and keep warm. On each bottom bun, spread Basil Mayonnaise, top with a burger, a slice of Camembert, some tomato, a few fried onions and the top of the bun. Serve and enjoy.

Ancho Chili Barbecue Sauce

Makes 8 cups (2 L)

The Ancho chili is a dried poblano chili that adds great flavour to a sauce. The heat level of this sauce is classified as mild—add more chilis, cayenne and black pepper to suit your individual taste. If the sauce is too thick, just add a little beer or water. You can also mix the sauce with apple cider at a 4:1 ratio, for a great mop to use on large cuts of meat to keep them moist.

2 onions, diced

¼ cup (60 mL) canola oil

2 Tbsp (30 mL) Dijon mustard

1 cup (250 mL) red wine vinegar

½ cup (125 mL) maple syrup

¼ cup (60 mL) capers

4 tsp (20 mL) hot sauce

1 Tbsp (15 mL) *each* paprika, cinnamon, coriander, allspice, ginger, oregano

1 x 1.25 L bottle of ketchup

1 Tbsp (15 mL) Ancho chili powder

1 tsp (5 mL) crushed red pepper flakes

1 Tbsp (15 mL) cracked black pepper

2 Tbsp (30 mL) Worcestershire sauce

In a large pan, brown onions well in the oil. Add remaining ingredients and simmer over low heat for 1 to 1½ hours, stirring occasionally to ensure no scorching. Remove from heat and cool to room temperature. Purée in a blender or with an immersion blender to desired consistency, and refrigerate.

Excellent with any grilled meat.

Tip

The sauce keeps for a few weeks in the refrigerator.

In recent decades immigrants from Central and South America have added to the rich cultural mosaic in Canada. People from El Salvador, for example, have settled in large cities such as Vancouver. Soccer is one event that has everyone on the streets in droves.

Strawberry Salsa

Makes 3 cups (750 mL)

June arrives and fresh strawberries start appearing in gardens, stores and farmers' markets across the country! This refreshing salsa goes well with any grilled chicken or grilled salmon. The sweetness of the strawberries blends with just a little heat to make a great combination of flavours. Try your own combination of seasonal fruit, such as blueberries, peaches and even mangoes—whatever taste you like! Just remember for presentation purposes to make sure that the berries are chopped the same size.

1 lb (500 g) strawberries, diced $\frac{1}{4}$ inch (0.5 cm)

1 Tbsp (15 mL) honey

1 Tbsp (15 mL) lemon juice

1 Tbsp (15 mL) Sambal Oelek (Asian chili sauce)

$\frac{1}{4}$ cup (60 mL) chopped fresh mint

$\frac{1}{4}$ cup (60 mL) sliced green onion

salt and pepper

Mix ingredients together a bowl and chill for at least 2 hours.

Great served over any grilled meat or fish.

 *Another influence of Central and South America and Mexico in Canadian cuisine is the wide variety of salsas that can range from fruity and spicy to tomato-based and richly flavoured.*

Argentinian Ukrainian Chimichurri Sauce

Makes 2½ cups (625 mL)

This recipe—basically, it's a salsa—is honestly one of my favourites. I make a batch and we use it on everything. You can marinate anything with it, mix it with mayonnaise for a great potato salad dressing, pour it on vegetables—you name it. This version is quite chunky; you can purée it in a food processor if you wish. It's called Argentinian Ukrainian Chimichurri Sauce because of the plentiful garlic, which is a feature of Ukrainian cooking. For the seasonings, always taste your recipe after you mix it—you are cooking for yourself, after all. It might need more salt, pepper, garlic...

¾ cup (175 mL) chopped fresh parsley

¼ cup (60 mL) chopped fresh garlic

2 Tbsp (30 mL) paprika

½ cup (125 mL) finely chopped onion

1 cup (250 mL) olive oil

¼ cup (60 mL) red wine vinegar

1 tsp (5 mL) chili powder

2 tsp (10 mL) dried oregano

1 tsp (5 mL) salt

½ tsp (2 mL) pepper

1 tsp (5 mL) or more hot sauce

2 Tbsp (30 mL) balsamic vinegar

Place ingredients in a jar. Cover and shake well. Adjust seasoning and allow to rest overnight before using.

Tip

The sauce will keep in the fridge for 3 weeks.

 *Freeze any leftovers and use them to add some summer pizzazz to braised dishes during the long winter.*

Roasted Tomato Salsa

Makes 4 cups (1 L)

Another multi-purpose salsa, this recipe goes well with any grilled meat. I use this salsa as a condiment throughout the year—finely chopped, it goes really well with nacho chips. Although I suggest using cherry, baby or grape tomatoes here, you can use any kind of tomato that you like, depending on the bounty of your garden or the farmers' market—just make sure the tomatoes are cut-side up when you put them on the barbecue.

2 lbs (1 kg) cherry, baby or grape tomatoes

½ cup (125 mL) extra-virgin olive oil

2 tsp (10 mL) kosher salt

1 tsp (5 mL) freshly cracked black pepper

about 2 tsp (10 mL) sugar

1 head garlic, cloves separated and peeled but left whole

Preheat the barbecue to medium. Cut tomatoes in half around the middle, not from stem to stem. Place cut-side up in a foil baking pan. Drizzle with olive oil, salt, pepper and a little sugar. Sprinkle as many whole garlic cloves as you like around and among tomatoes. The garlic will flavour the olive oil and the juices created as the tomatoes roast more than the actual tomatoes.

Place on the grill and close the lid of the barbecue. Roast for about 30 to 45 minutes, or until tomatoes start to burst though their skins. Remove from pan and let cool.

Tip

Use this salsa for pasta sauce, on bruschetta or as a vinaigrette. It's also a tasty addition to other dishes such as soups and stews.

Leamington, Ontario, is the Tomato Capital of Canada. You'd be surprised at all the tomato-related activities here—but the point is that the area produces great tomatoes.

Fajita Marinade

Makes 3 cups (750 mL)

Mexico is one of the most popular tourist destinations for snowbirds, whether it's Cancun or Puerto Vallarta. My brother-in-law Brian got this recipe in Mexico from some guy named Oscar. It's great with a flank steak or sirloin, but also works with chicken. The ingredient volumes may seem a little odd, but they work. Make sure you marinate the meat for at least 12 hours.

2 cups (500 mL) bottled Italian dressing

1 Tbsp (15 mL) hot sauce

$\frac{1}{4}$ cup (60 mL) seasoning salt

1 Tbsp (15 mL) freshly cracked black pepper

1 Tbsp (15 mL) cumin

1 Tbsp (15 mL) liquid smoke (see Tip)

2 Tbsp (30 mL) lime juice

2 tsp (10 mL) Worcestershire sauce

2 Tbsp (30 mL) canola oil

Mix ingredients together in a medium bowl. Place in a larger bowl or sealable plastic bag with meat. Refrigerate for 12 hours or overnight.

Remove meat from marinade; discard marinade. Remember to pat meat dry before grilling.

Tip

Liquid smoke is a condiment that adds a smoky piquance to food. It's available in any grocery store near the ketchups, mustards and barbecue sauces.

Pomegranate Vinaigrette

Makes 1½ cups (375 mL)

We usually think that vinaigrettes go with salads, but the combination of flavours in this easy recipe make it a great complement to grilled meat. I drizzle this vinaigrette over chicken and fish, and it goes particularly well with the Pistachio-dusted Leg of Lamb (p. 114). You can simply mix up a batch in a small glass jar and leave it in the fridge.

juice and seeds from 1 pomegranate

2 Tbsp (30 mL) red wine vinegar

2 Tbsp (30 mL) pomegranate molasses (see Tip)

1 Tbsp (15 mL) Dijon mustard

½ cup (125 mL) extra-virgin olive oil

salt and pepper

Squeeze pomegranate juice and seeds into a medium bowl; be careful not to get any pulp in the bowl or juice on yourself (it can stain clothing). Add vinegar and whisk in molasses and Dijon mustard. Once well combined, drizzle olive oil in slowly while whisking. Season with salt and pepper and adjust the seasoning to taste.

Serve on a salad of field greens with slivered red onions and toasted pecans. For a different twist, try slightly heating the dressing before pouring it over the salad.

Tip

Before you ever dress a salad, be sure to season the greens with salt and pepper.

Tip

Pomegranate molasses is available at most grocery stores. Pomegranates themselves are available in grocery stores in Canada from November through to around Christmas.

Green Pea Guacamole

Makes 3 cups (750 mL)

Everyone knows that guacamole is made with avocados, but I think this recipe, using peas instead, is a really neat idea. It's a way out recipe—probably the farthest way out recipe in this book, but try it. It's tasty and low in fat, and it's something different to try with quesadillas or nachos as you sit and watch the rest of your meal cook on the barbecue. And you can use your own summer bounty of home-grown peas in this recipe.

2 cups (500 mL) frozen green peas, defrosted

½ cup (125 mL) extra-virgin olive oil

juice and zest from 1 lime

¼ cup (60 mL) finely diced red onion

2 Tbsp (30 mL) chopped fresh cilantro

salt and pepper

Place peas in a food processor, and pulse 5 times just to break them up. With the processor on, add olive oil, lime zest and juice; and process until combined. Pour the mixture into a medium bowl and add onion and cilantro. Add salt and pepper as desired.

Serve just as you would normal guacamole.

Bagna Cadu

Makes 2½ cups (625 mL)

Here's another great classic Italian recipe perfect for the grilling season. This warm anchovy garlic bath goes well with grilled vegetables, as a dip or napped over a piece of grilled fish or meat. Do not let the anchovies scare you away—they mellow and offer a soft, salty, rich flavour.

½ cup (125 mL) butter

1 head garlic, roasted (see p. 12) and crushed

2 tins anchovies, mashed

2 cups (500 mL) extra-virgin olive oil

salt and pepper

juice from 1 lemon

Heat butter in a saucepan on the side burner over low heat. Once the butter has melted, add garlic and cook for 3 minutes. Form a paste by adding the anchovies. Drizzle with olive oil, and season with salt and pepper and lemon juice. Pour into a fondue pot and keep warm. Serve with raw fresh vegetables and bread for dipping.

Eighty percent of Canada's Italian population lives in Ontario, but the far-reaching influences of Italian cuisine can be felt from sea to sea.

Smoked Salmon

Serves 8 to 10 as an appetizer

The salmon in this recipe is smoked using the hot smoke method, in which the heat is over 200° F (95° C). Try to find some wild Atlantic salmon for this dish: it has a higher fat content and smokes well. You can use any type of wood to perfume the salmon, as long as it is a hardwood. Stay away from pine and softwoods—the smoke they create is not pleasant.

Cure

¼ cup (60 mL) brown sugar

¼ cup (60 mL) kosher salt

1 tsp (5 mL) chopped rosemary

Smoked Salmon

plastic wrap

1 x 1 to 1½ lb (500 to 750 g) salmon fillet

1 cup (250 mL) apple wood chips

heavy foil

Mix cure ingredients together in a small bowl and set aside.

Lay down two pieces of plastic wrap, making sure they overlap. Spread half of the cure mixture on the wrap, and place the salmon, skin-side down, on top. Spread the rest of the cure on the salmon, making sure you cover the fish. Wrap salmon in plastic wrap and then wrap once more. Place on a baking sheet, and refrigerate for 4 hours, flipping once. Remove fish, rinse well and pat dry.

Preheat one side of the barbecue to medium, and leave the other side off. Place the wood chips in the middle of a square sheet of heavy foil. Bring the corners together to make a pouch, and poke several holes in the foil. Place over the burner of the barbecue. When smoke starts appearing from the foil pouch, place salmon on the off side of the barbecue. Maintain temperature at no higher than 300° F (150° C). You want the fish to reach an internal temperature of 140° F (60° C), and when it does, remove to a platter and serve immediately, or chill and serve later.

Smoked Fennel Trout

Serves 8

Any recipe worth its salt offers intriguing tastes and a satisfying outcome. This brined trout dish from Company's Coming, flavoured with fennel seed and lemon, will reward your culinary curiosity on both counts. If you're wondering about the brining technique, immersing fish in a higher-concentration salt solution allows the fish to be infused by the flavours it contained. When cooked, brined fish retains much of this moisture.

4 x 8 oz (225 g) whole rainbow trout, pan-ready

Brine

4 cups (1 L) water)

1 cup (250 mL) chopped onion

2/3 cup (150 mL) coarse salt

2 Tbsp (30 mL) fennel seed, crushed

2 cloves garlic, minced

2 tsp (10 mL) fennel seed, crushed

8 lemon slices, halved

2 cups (500 mL) apple wood chips, soaked in water for 1 hour and drained

1 Tbsp (15 mL) fennel seed, soaked in water for 1 hour and drained

Stir brine ingredients in 9 x 13 inch (23 x 33 cm) baking dish until salt is dissolved. Add fish and cover with plastic wrap. Set a cutting board over top and use a weight to keep fish submerged in brine. Chill for 1 hour. Drain and discard brine. Rinse fish and pat dry.

Sprinkle second amount of fennel seed in cavity of fish and fill with lemon slices.

Put wood chips and third amount of fennel seed into smoker box. Place smoker box on one barbecue burner and turn it on to high. Once box begins to smoke, adjust burner temperature to achieve internal barbecue temperature of medium-high. Cook fish over unlit burner for about 10 minutes per side until it flakes easily when tested with a fork.

This dish is also delicious served cold.

Smoked Pork Loin

Serves 6

This is a forgiving recipe, so it's a good choice to start with when you begin to enjoy the rewards of smoking meat. The true key here is the brine, which will add flavour and moisture to the meat while it is smoking. Use this recipe as a base and then add the flavours that you like.

1 x 3 lb (1.5 kg) pork loin

2 cups (500 mL) apple or cherry wood chips

heavy foil

Brine
¼ cup (60 mL) kosher salt

¼ cup (60 mL) brown sugar

¼ cup (60 mL) paprika

2 tsp (10 mL) garlic powder

2 tsp (10 mL) dried oregano

4 cups (1 L) water

Place the brine ingredients in a large pot. Bring to a boil and simmer for 5 minutes. Remove from heat, chill to room temperature and then chill to ice cold.

Put pork in the brine and refrigerate for 1 hour per pound of meat. Once the meat has been in the brine for the allotted time, remove and rinse well with cold water, pat dry and set aside. Discard brine.

Place 1 cup (250 mL) of wood chips in the middle of a square sheet of foil. Bring the corners together to make a pouch; poke several holes in pouch. Make a second pouch the same way with remaining wood chips.

Preheat one side of the barbecue to medium and leave the other side off. Place the pouch on the heated side. When smoke starts seeping out of the pouch, place the pork loin on the off side of the barbecue and close the lid. Maintain a temperature no higher than 300° F (150° C), and try not to open the lid. After 45 minutes, replace the first pouch with the second, and continue to smoke meat for another 45 minutes, or until the internal temperature is above 145° F (63° C). Let meat relax, slice and enjoy.

This pork makes the best Rueben sandwich you've ever eaten, especially if you're lucky enough to have some of Mrs. Kuhlmann's sauerkraut. Look it up if you don't believe me.

Orange Chili-stuffed Pork Chops

Serves 4

You'll find deliciously duelling sources of heat in these Italian sausage-stuffed pork chops from the Company's Coming kitchen. The smoke from the apple wood chips and the sweetness of the glaze also combine for a meaty, flavourful experience.

4 bone-in pork rib chops, about 1½ inches (4 cm) thick, trimmed of fat

salt and pepper

Stuffing

2 tsp (10 mL) canola oil

¾ lb (340 g) hot Italian sausage, casing removed

1 cup (250 mL) chopped onion

2 cloves garlic, minced

½ cup (125 mL) diced red pepper

½ cup (125 mL) sweet chili sauce

2 tsp (10 mL) grated orange zest

2 cups (500 mL) apple wood chips, soaked in water for 1 hour and drained

Heat canola oil in a frying pan on medium high. Add sausage, onion and garlic and scramble-fry until sausage is no longer pink. Add red pepper and scramble-fry until tender-crisp. Remove pan from heat and let stand until cool.

Cut slits horizontally in pork chops to create pockets. Fill with stuffing and secure with wooden picks. Sprinkle with salt and pepper.

Combine chili sauce and orange zest.

Put wood chips into smoker box. Place smoker box on one barbecue burner and turn it on to high. Once box begins to smoke, adjust burner temperature to achieve internal barbecue temperature of medium. Cook pork chops over unlit burner for about 25 minutes per side, brushing occasionally with chili sauce mixture, until internal temperature of pork reaches 160° F (71° C). Cover with foil and let stand for 5 minutes. Remove picks before serving.

Tip

The filling can be made a day ahead, but the chops should be stuffed just before they are cooked.

Tip

To find chops that are the required thickness, you may have to make a special request of your butcher.

Smoked Strip Loin

Serves 6 to 8

I love smoked beef—it has a fantastic flavour, and it's good hot or cold, sliced thin or thick. You can prepare this recipe for a large party—it will really showcase your culinary skills around the barbecue. I prefer strip loin, but any tender cut of beef can be used.

1 x 4 to 5 lb (2 to 2.3 kg) strip loin roast

1 cup (250 mL) Barbecue Rub (p. 56) or your favourite spice mix

3 cups (750 mL) cherry wood chips

heavy foil

Pat the meat dry, then coat with rub or spice mix, making sure you get some rub in all creases and folds. Put roast in a baking dish and refrigerate at least 6 hours.

Place 1 cup (250 mL) of wood chips in middle of a square sheet of foil. Fold the corners together to form a pouch; poke several holes in the pouch. Make 2 more pouches with remaining wood chips.

Preheat the barbecue to medium on one side and leave the other side off. Retrieve the roast from the fridge. Place a pouch on the heated side of the barbecue. Once smoke starts curling out of the pouch, place strip loin roast on the off side of the barbecue. Close the lid and let cook for 45 minutes.

Switch pouches and continue to smoke for another 45 minutes. Check to see if the meat is cooked—an internal temperature of 130° F (54° C) means the meat is rare. If not, put the third pouch into the barbecue and cook roast until desired doneness is reached. When cooked, allow meat to relax for 15 minutes before carving.

The wood chips used in these smoking recipes tend to be apple or cherry because they are abundantly available in many parts of Canada. Bags of more exotic hardwoods, such imported pecan and hickory, are available in places that stock barbecue equipment and will subtly alter the final flavour of this recipe.

Smoked Tomatoes

Makes 4 cups (1 L)

Summer tomatoes are the best tomatoes of the year, and with a slight smoky flavour, they're even better. These tomatoes can be used in vinaigrettes or dressings, relishes and salsas, or in place of fresh or sun-dried tomatoes.

2 lbs (1 kg) tomatoes

salt and pepper

½ cup (125 mL) hardwood chips

heavy foil

Slice the tomatoes in half horizontally, not from stem to stem. Squeeze the seeds out and place tomato halves, cut-side up, on a wire rack set on a foil baking sheet. Season to taste with salt and pepper.

Place wood chips in middle of a square sheet of foil, bring the corners together and make a pouch. Poke several holes in pouch.

Preheat one side of the barbecue to medium-low and leave the other side off. Place the pouch on the hot side of the barbecue. When smoke starts appearing from the pouch, place tomatoes on the off side of the barbecue. Close the lid and maintain a temperature of 200° F (95° C) or less for 30 minutes. When the tomatoes are cooked, take them off the barbecue and pull the skins off. Chop or use whole—just be sure to use the accumulated liquid as well.

The tomato is another food product that originated in the Americas. It was brought to Europe by explorers and was originally treated with suspicion. Nowadays Canadians should treat the tasteless, woody tomatoes on store shelves in January with suspicion. Instead, smoke your own summer tomatoes to last you through the long winter.

Maple-smoked Chicken Breast

Serves 6 to 8

Smoked chicken breasts are great hot or cold, and they're equally great in a chicken salad. Chicken breasts are very versatile, and this recipe is another delicious way to cook them. Because chicken is so lean, the breasts will dry out if you overcook them. I think maple goes well in this dish—and it's a quintessentially Canadian ingredient we should feel justly proud of—but feel free to use honey, molasses or your favourite sweetener.

6 to 8 boneless chicken breasts, skin-on optional

Brine

¼ cup (60 mL) kosher salt

¼ cup (60 mL) maple syrup

1 cinnamon stick

4 cups (1 L) water

1 cup (250 mL) hardwood chips

heavy foil

Place the salt, maple syrup, cinnamon stick and water in a medium pot. Bring to a boil and simmer for 10 minutes. Chill to room temperature, then refrigerate until ice cold. Add the chicken breast and refrigerate for 1 hour per pound (½ hour per kg) of meat.

Remove chicken from brine, rinse well with cold water and pat dry. Discard brine.

Place wood chips in middle of a square sheet of foil. Bring corners together to make a pouch. Poke several holes in pouch.

Preheat one side of the barbecue to medium-low; leave the other side off. Put the pouch on the heated side. When smoke starts to appear from the pouch, place the chicken breast on the off side of the barbecue. Close the lid and smoke 30 minutes, maintaining a temperature of 300° F (150° C) or less, until chicken is cooked.

Great for a different twist in Thai spring rolls instead of pork.

Smoked Whole Chicken

Serves 4

Rich golden brown colour on the outside, and tender, moist and juicy on the inside—this is chicken cooked the easy way, with no flare-ups, turning or watching. Simply season and smoke—what could be easier? You could use the brine given for the Maple-smoked Chicken Breast (p. 146), but to keep it easy, I just make a simple rub. Organic chicken is widely available now; make the effort to find local sources.

1 x 3 lb (1.5 kg) broiler chicken

¼ cup (60 mL) seasoning salt

2 Tbsp (30 mL) brown sugar

2 cups (500 mL) hardwood chips

heavy foil

Mix the salt and sugar together in a small bowl, then rub over entire bird. Place chicken in a baking dish and refrigerate for at least 1 hour.

Place half of the wood chips in the middle of a square sheet of foil. Bring the corners together and make a pouch. Make a second pouch with the remaining chips. Poke several holes in each pouch.

Preheat one side of the barbecue to medium-low and leave the other side off. Place one pouch on the heated side of the barbecue. When smoke starts curling out of the pouch, place chicken on the off side. Close the lid and smoke for 90 minutes, maintaining a temperature of 300° F (150° C) or less. Switch pouches after 45 minutes. When the chicken is cooked, remove and let rest 15 minutes, and then carve.

You'll never rotisserie chicken again after you've tasted this dish. To shorten cooking time, you can split the bird.

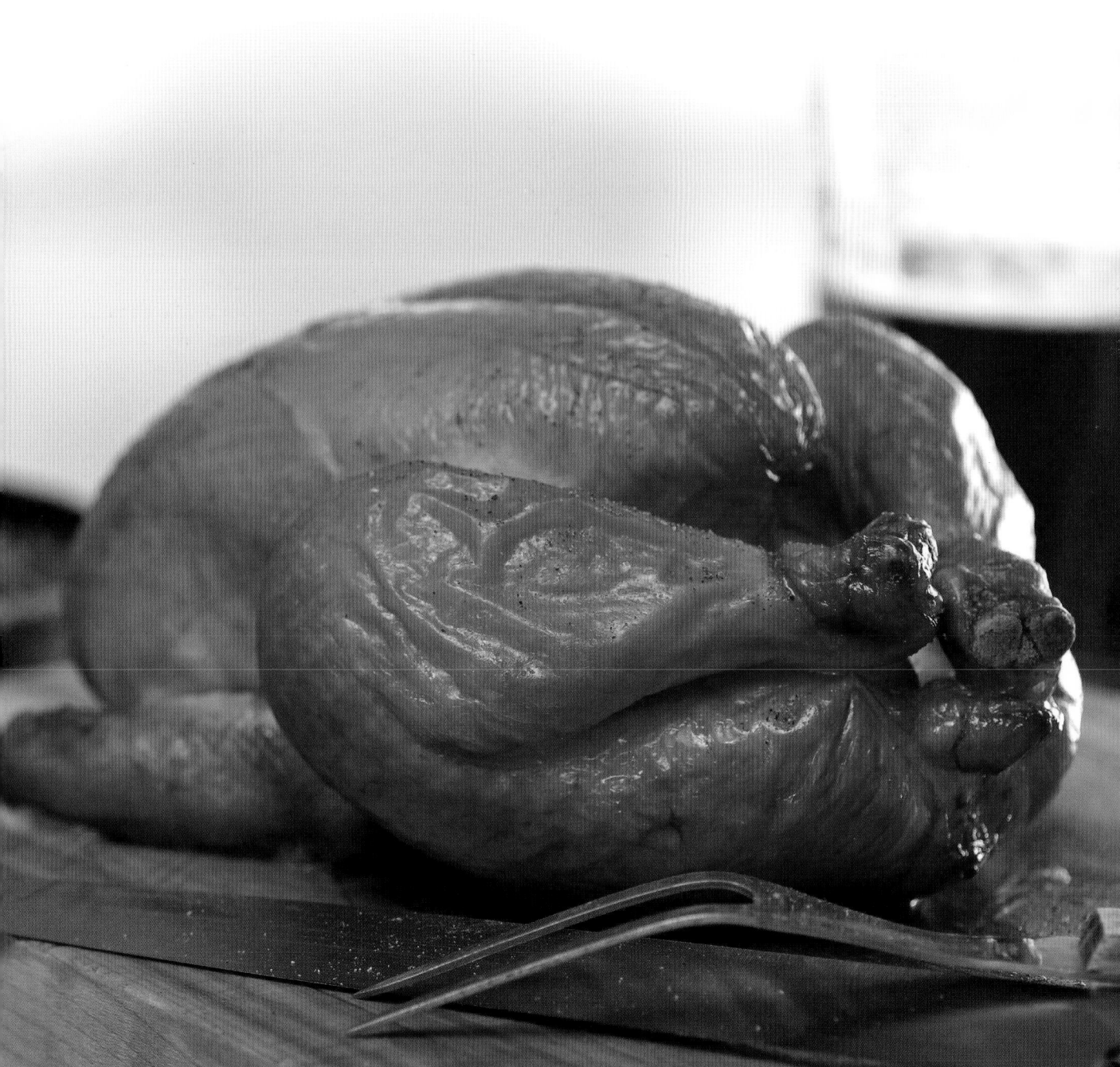

Maple Bacon Sundae

Serves 6

This recipe was inspired by my friend Jane, who is an awesome home cook. She served a dish like this at her Canada Day celebration with great success. Later, in August, I served it to a news anchor and friends from Tuscany, also to rave reviews. Is there anything that could be more Canadian?

1 cup maple syrup

½ cup cooked, crispy double-smoked bacon (not burnt), crumbled

½ cup chopped pecans or your favourite nuts

vanilla ice cream for a crowd

Put syrup in saucepan and bring to a boil; let cook to reduce a little. Add bacon crumbles and give it a good stir. Add nuts and remove from heat. I like to let the sauce sit for a while.

When you're ready, spoon a couple of blobs of ice cream on each dish and top with sauce. Yum yum.

The sweet familiarity of the maple syrup combines so well with the saltiness of the bacon, the crunchiness of the nuts and the cold ice cream. Your family is going to love this. I like Bourbon Vanilla or Rye Vanilla ice cream if you can find it.

Grilled Bananas

Serves 4

These grilled bananas make for a fabulous dessert. This recipe presents a unique combination of flavours—bananas, sugar and chili—which are then drizzled with chocolate. The blend of textures and flavours works well together: just think of the crunchy sweetness of the sugar, the tang of the chili, and the softness of the bananas. Use other types of fruit instead of bananas, if you like.

½ cup (125 mL) white sugar

1 Tbsp (15 mL) chili powder

4 bananas

1 cup (250 mL) chocolate sauce

In a small bowl, mix the sugar and the chili powder. Set aside.

Preheat the barbecue to medium-low. Cut bananas in half lengthwise, then width-wise, but do not peel. Dip cut side of bananas into the sugar–chili powder mixture, making sure that they are well coated.

Grill bananas cut-side down until the sugar starts to caramelize. Place each banana on a plate, and let sugar harden as it cools slightly. Then peel bananas, drizzle them with chocolate sauce and serve.

Fall Fruit Hash

Serves 4

A great dessert on a cool fall evening combines fruit from the Okanagan with Quebec maple syrup. All the cooking for this dessert can be done in a cast iron pan on the barbecue. You can use any flavour of ice cream, and you can either make the waffles yourself or buy them.

2 Tbsp (30 mL) butter

2 cups (500 mL) diced apples

2 cups (500 mL) diced pears

½ cup (125 mL) pure maple syrup

¼ cup (60 mL) dried cranberries

½ tsp (2 mL) cinnamon

4 waffles, homemade or purchased

ice cream

Preheat the barbecue to medium. Melt butter in a cast iron pan on the grill. Once the foam has subsided, add apple, pear and maple syrup. Slowly simmer for about 10 minutes, until the fruit is fork tender and the sauce is reduced. Add cranberries and cinnamon.

Reheat waffles on grill until golden brown and crispy, and then cut in half. Place ½ waffle on each of 4 plates. Divide fruit on top, and top with remaining waffle halves. Serve with a spoonful of ice cream, and drizzle with any remaining sauce from the pan.

 *Leftover fruit goes great with grilled pork or poultry.*

Spiced Grilled Peaches

Serves 4

It's so appropriate to end a barbecue meal with a dessert that you've just cooked up on the grill. Grilling fruit only heightens its natural sweetness. This recipe from the Company's Coming collection features fresh peaches coated in a sweet and spicy glaze. Serve with ice cream or whipped cream and a garnish of berries on the side.

1 cup (250 mL) water

¾ cup (175 mL) liquid honey

½ tsp (2 mL) ground cinnamon

½ tsp (2 mL) ground ginger

¼ tsp (1 mL) ground cardamom

⅛ tsp (0.5 mL) pepper

¼ tsp (1 mL) vanilla extract

6 fresh peaches, halved and pits removed (see Tip)

Combine water, honey, cinnamon, ginger, cardamom and pepper in small saucepan. Bring to a boil. Reduce heat to medium. Simmer, uncovered, for about 22 minutes until reduced to about ¾ cup (175 mL). Reserve ⅓ cup (75 mL) honey mixture in small heatproof bowl.

Add vanilla to honey mixture in small bowl. Stir. Pour remaining honey mixture into large bowl.

Add peaches. Stir until coated. Let stand for 10 minutes. Preheat barbecue to medium. Remove peaches from honey mixture. Place on greased grill. Close lid. Cook peaches for about 3 minutes per side, brushing occasionally with honey mixture, until grill marks appear. Discard any remaining honey mixture. Transfer to serving plate. Drizzle with reserved vanilla mixture.

Tip

Wash peaches thoroughly before cutting to remove the majority of the "fuzz." Keeping the skin on helps the peaches stay intact while cooking.

Index

ABOUT THE AUTHORS

Brad Smoliak owns Brad Smoliak Cooks, an Edmonton-based company dedicated to developing, testing and bringing to market menus, recipes and new food products for restaurants, food manufacturers and foodservice providers. Brad blends his 25 years of culinary training as an executive chef with a knowledge of food science and clear business acumen to create food products that taste great and meet the needs of food consumers. Brad has created foods and recipes for a wide variety of clients across Canada and North America.

Brad was the Lead Consulting Chef for the Alberta government in its promotional efforts at the 2010 Vancouver Olympics. Brad developed and oversaw the execution of the menus for Alberta House and the Alberta-branded train between Vancouver and Whistler, using all Alberta-based products. Through Brad's culinary creativity, the Alberta advantage and brand truly came to life. Brad was the executive chef and one of the founders of Hardware Grill in Edmonton, often cited as one of Canada's top 10 restaurants. Brad also served as the executive chef for the Royal Mayfair Golf & Country Club and Normand's Restaurant, and also had the opportunity to cook for Queen Elizabeth II when she visited in 2005.

Brad is a Certified Research Chef and has advanced his knowledge and skills with ongoing training and development at the Guelph Food and Technology Centre and the Culinary Institute of America at Greystone in California. Brad is also a frequent guest chef on many television news shows and has supplied articles and recipes for several food publications.

Brad makes his home in Edmonton with his wife Leanne, who is also a trained chef, his son Nicholas (already a well-established foodie at the age of 17) and their dog Cosmo.

Jean Paré started her official culinary career as a caterer in Vermilion, Alberta, before going on to found Company's Coming and become Canada's most popular cookbook author—selling 30 million books! Her story appears on p. 4.